BLACKMA

By

Michelle Jean

It's November 07, 2013 and I thought I was done with the Michelle Jean line of books for a while but unfortunately I am not done. Good God does not want me to be done for some strange reason.

Yes there is much more to come hence this book on Spiritual war.

I have to talk about spiritual war because the spiritual forces have become deadly. I have to tell you what is to come and or what is brewing in the spiritual realm right now hence the picture of spaceships that is on the first page of this book.

People especially you White People. Good luck to your race in the spiritual world because you are doomed but not entirely.

We talk about heaven and earth and everyone has and have forgotten about spiritual warfare. We say we want to go to heaven but I tell you, ***STRIVE NOT TO BE IN HEAVEN.***

STRIVE TO BE IN THE ABODE OF GOOD GOD.

I repeat, STRIVE TO BE IN THE ABODE OF GOOD GOD because _heaven is no different from earth._

There is death in heaven and this death you will not escape. _Hence I tell humanity to live by truth because we were told, truth is everlasting life._

I've told you, _the goodness that you do you can take it with you up to see and live with Good God._ **_But the evils that you do, you must go to hell and die._** There are no ands ifs or buts about this. This is the reality of every human being that is on the face of this planet. This is also the reality of everyone that is dead. _**If they did not live a good and clean life on earth there triangle cannot go up it must go down.**_ _This is the law and no one can change this thus saith the Lord thy God. Meaning it is so._

This morning, November 07 2013, I dreamt I was watching not participating in the killing of White People hence this book.

It was as if I was on another planet and this is what I saw. I saw spaceships. The spaceships look like the H spaceships on page one of this book and they were neatly aligned. There were many of them and they were small. All of a sudden they opened fire and started killing White People. Please note there were no black people in this dream accept for me. I was a spectator watching the destruction take place like I said. White people were dying and this huge ship was there but I cannot describe the huge ship to you. All I know is a window opened and this white lady stretched forth her hand and started to lift people in her spaceship. The first one to get in the ship was a white man. She managed to save a few and escaped with them to another dimension. I call it another dimension but even with her saving some of the people and the escaped she escaped with them to another dimension, they were not safe. In the dream she (the lady of the huge spaceship) had this compact that looked like a powder compact. You know what, let me go to Google and see if I can find the image for you to see what I'm talking about. Go to Google Images and type in Powder Puff Makeup. The compact that this lady had is exactly like the powder puff in the second row. The first compact in the second row which is the 400 X 455 robertjonesb. This is the exact compact the lady had expect, the compact was square not round. She threw it out the window. Upon throwing the compact out the window it detonated. Meaning it blew up some of the H spaceships. And note this is prior to them escaping to another dimension or universe for some. And yes people I write like I sound, meaning my thought are in Patwa or Patois sometimes, hence my English may be weird or nonsensical to some of you, but please bare with me.

This dream is weird to some but sane to me because I've told you, ***skin color is crap in many senses.***

Black Skin represents PHYSICAL DEATH AND White Skin represents SPIRITUAL DEATH.

This you should know already if you've read any of my prior books. So when you the white race say your skin is superior to the black skin, I laugh because you are true sin - death. ***Meaning your skin is spiritual death – final death and all who is evil die like you.*** Meaning when evil dies, they die as a white person dressed in white. *So the seeing of all White People dying just means I am seeing the death of sin and his sinful and wicked race of people.*

HENCE BLACK INFINITELY AND INDEFINITELY FOREVER EVER CANNOT DIE BECAUSE BLACK IS THE BANNER OF GOOD GOD AND WHITE IS THE TRUE AND EVERLASTING BANNER OF DEATH AND HIS PEOPLE.

This is why many of you say you are superior to the black race but you can never be superior to the black race.

DEATH IS DEATH AS DEATH WILL BE DEATH HENCE DEATH CAN INFINITELY AND

INDEFINITELY NEVER EVER BE SUPERIOR TO LIFE – GOOD LIFE.

BLACK IS GOOD LIFE HENCE IT IS THE BANNER OF EVERLASTING LIFE AS WELL AS GOOD GOD.

You are the dead ones hence many of you rape and steal lands that do not belong to you.

Many of you steal the wealth of nations and reduce them to rubble while leaving them penniless and hungry and your land and people's bellies are full.

Many of you wage war against other lands and kill – take innocent lives for what does not belong to you.

Many of you create diseases and bring them to other countries – lands to wipe out their people so you can steal the resources of that nation including their land.

Many of you write books of lies especially the whoring and sinful book you call the holy bible to deceive nations and bring them to hell with you. While doing this you steal their land and defile it with your false gods of death and deceit. You rape them of their wealth and give them the gods to death to kill their spirit and rob them of the TRUE AND LIVING GOD – GOOD GOD.

Many of you condemn the black race but yet feed them lies about your deceiving BLACK JESUS. Yes some of you say White Jesus but according to your book of Sin, Revelations 1 depict Jesus as black. Yes Jesus – Zeus the frauds that never existed. Pegasus existed but not Zeus and I've told you who Pegasus represents hence the white race riding off the coattails of the black race. And yes you can say White death riding on the Coattail of Black Death and now it's time for WHITE DEATH TO BE KICKED OFF INFINITELY AND INDEFINITELY. It's time the black man truly reclaim his birthright which is life – good life. Yes you can say I am racist here but the truth is the truth. You cannot take another man's heritage and claim it as your own. Right is right and wrong is wrong and I truly don't give a damn if anyone is offended. If the shoe was on the other foot you too would say the same. I refuse to be a hypocrite like many in society hence I walk alone on the road of Good God without man – anyone (human) preaching to me and telling me lies.

You are the regressive Nigga's that we must separate from, hence Marcus Mosiah Garvey and his teachings. Black is superior to White. Hence Black in its pure and true state is true and everlasting, forever ever and eternal life not white. White is blinding hence no one can comprehend the darkness – void as you call it. And if you take this on a skin tone level, know that you are a nigger void of comprehension of true and good life. Hence if you do not know the spiritual realm then shut the hell up because you truly know nothing.

Now with all that said, many of you are saying what a racist so and so but if you are true to Good God and me and if you've read any of my other books then you would not let the words above phase you or make you feel out of place.

If you do then you have a problem because I've specifically told you that some Whites and Chinese fall under the banner of Black and some Blacks fall under the banner of White. The banner of Black does not have anything to do with skin colour but has everything to do with your goodness and truth.

You were told truth is everlasting life so if you do not live by goodness and truth you cannot have everlasting life. And no, it does not mean that you have to like everybody because I don't like everybody. Some nations I don't want to step foot in their lands because it is forbidden unto me. And yes due to Ancestral thwarting or blood, I am the way I am to a large extent. Know that I cannot fully explain ancestral blood but truly know that it runs through my veins. I have to in many ways vindicate my ancestors and Good God knows this. I also have to vindicate Good God and he knows this as well.

Onwards I Go because this book is entitled Blackman Redemption – Spiritual War.

Spiritual war is real because we all know that as it is in heaven so it is on earth. So if there is fighting on earth there must be fighting in the spiritual realm and I've tried to show you this.

Like I said, no one can blame God or the devil for what's happening on earth because we are the ones to buy into the bullshit of the devil and his lying and deceiving people. I can blame God and I can blame the devil because I know what I can blame them for.

There are no gods in the physical and spiritual just Good and Evil hence BLACK AND WHITE. BLACK DEATH IN THE PHYSICAL AND WHITE DEATH IN THE SPIRITUAL.

We are the ones to refuse to go to God and ask him directly about things. And know that God – Good God does not reside in the spiritual realm.

Now the spiritual realm has waged war on the White Race because like I said, I did not see one black person in all of this. And although some white people got saved it did not mean that they were safe.

Death was still on their tail. Like I've said and will forever tell humanity, the death of flesh is nothing compared to spiritual death. *Spiritual death is true death – the death of life not the death of flesh. Spiritual death is your final death.* You cannot be resurrected because life cannot be resurrected. If you are evil you are going to die a painful death. If you are good you will move up to see Good God and Good Life. Meaning you will reside with Goof God. This is the law thus saith the Lord thy God, meaning it is so. The flesh goes back to Mother Earth because the spirit became earthly due to the sins of man – humanity. Meaning we accept blood and not water – the pure waters of Good God. Because of this evil – wicked and evil people have us fighting and buying death – a place in hell. And this is why I keep telling you and will forever tell you, *YOU CANNOT BUY LIFE YOU CAN ONLY BUY DEATH.* Good God gave us good life and we are to live a good and clean life on earth so that when the spirit shed the flesh, it can go directly to Good God in his abode which is not paradise or heaven. Paradise and heaven is hell because Muslims kill to get there. Hence they tell you when they kill they go directly to paradise to see their god who is death. They don't tell you this but Good God is telling you the truth. So truly listen because despite our dirty ways Good God and or God has and have been trying to help us. Know that Christians die to get to heaven because they say Jesus die for their sins and through the shedding of blood their sins will be remitted. They do this but forgot the law that says, "THOU SHALT NOT KILL." So if you shed blood how can you go up to see Good God?

If you wallow in the nastiness of religion, how can Good God save you or even forgive you?

Its 4:50 AM family and I can't go back to sleep. I just had a dream that I was tossed in jail by the Aryans for my books. Wow this deadly society that thinks if you do not have blonde hair and blue eyes with a lighter hue of white skin you are not pure.

In the dream this racist attitude or the Aryans were also of Spanish background. I can't remember if the Spanish in the dream were Colombian but they were White Spanish.

So to the Aryan Nation – the White Nation whether Spanish, African, Caribbean let me echo this. **_NO WEAPON OR WEAPONS FORMED AGAINST ME SHALL PROSPER._** Because the lock you locked me up, Good God released me. Hence I refuse to be your Daniel in your lion's den and Good God will not let this happen to me. So no matter what you the Aryan Nation do, you will never succeed. What you do to flesh you cannot do to spirit because when my flesh go back to Mother Earth **_MY SPIRIT WILL RISE_**

UP TO GOOD GOD BECAUSE THE UPRIGHT TRIANGLE IS A SEAL – THE SEAL OF LIFE – GOOD LIFE AND I HAVE THE SEAL OF LIFE LITERALLY.

Duly remember the dream above because like I said, it was not the black race that the spaceships opened fire on BUT THE WHITE RACE.

God – Good God cannot kill his own. Death kills his own hence from the dream yesterday and today none of you are God's own. *Thus I will say it again. ON THE MOUNTAIN OF GOD – GOOD GOD, I ONLY SAW ONE WHITE PERSON. I DID NOT SEE ANY INDIANS OR SPANISH PEOPLE so tell me now, if this is the case, WHAT SAY YOU TO GOOD GOD BECAUSE NONE OF YOU ARE INCLUDED ON THE MOUNTAIN OF GOOD GOD EXCEPT FOR THAT ONE WHITE PERSON. I know I know, there could be more and is more but I want to get my point across.*

No matter what you do to kill the black race, you will never succeed because God – Good God is black and he will never change to suit your race or any given race.

Yes the dream also had to do with Jesus – your Christos. Because in the dream I clearly stated Jesus was black, this according to your book of sin. In the dream the Black man that went to Princeton saved me meaning took me out of jail. As soon as I was jailed he was right there to release me. He said to me, he always thought Jesus to be black but he did not know he was. I told him Revelations One gives you the description of Jesus as being black. ***But I did not get a chance to tell him that Jesus did not exist.*** There were two white children in the dream and they too did not know that Jesus was black. When I told them it's in their bible they too could not believe that that passage existed in Revelations. I told them including the black man that released me from jail that the passage said Jesus had feet like burnt brass, hair like wool. I didn't get far in the description but the girl had a change of heart, meaning she now knew the truth but the boy would not accept the truth. In truth it matters not whether the white race accepts the truth or not because at the end of the day Good God is whom that matters and no weapon and weapons formed against his children shall prosper.

Like I've said before and will say again, NO RACE ON THE FACE OF THE PLANET IT PURE. ABSOLUTELY NONE BECAUSE WE ALL HAVE SIN IN US. HENCE WE ARE DEATH'S CHILDREN BECAUSE BOTH RACES – THE WHITE AND BLACK RACE REPRESENT DEATH. BLACK PEOPLE REPRESENT PHYSICAL DEATH AND THE WHITE RACE REPRESENT SPIRITUAL DEATH OR FINAL DEATH.

So to the Aryan Nation of sin and evil, none of you represent life. You all represent death. None of you know the representation of the colour blue because blue is used by both good and evil depending on the darkness of the colour. So truly get over yourself because like I said, BLACK is superior to WHITE. IT WAS A BLACK GOD THAT CREATED THIS UNIVERSE AS WELL AS YOUR RACIST ASS. So get over yourself because every living and breathing organism that hath life, has black in them, including you hence the different hues in life.

There is no escape for your racist ass. And no matter the white lady saving some of you, your race was not safe where she brought you.

__As for you the African race, I will not tell you again to smarten the hell up. None of you represent THE TRUE LIFE AND WAY OF YOUR ANCESTORS. If you all did, AFRICA WOULD NOT BE IN SUCH DISARRAY TODAY.__

What the hell are you fighting for?

What the hell are you disrespecting land, culture, heritage and self for?

You are Africans – Nubians but yet you act like colonized slaves and refuse to throw away the slave man mentality. Stop disrespecting Good God and his hue because he did make you like him.

Tell me something. You are Africans but yet you are fighting for the white man religion – the religion of the dead.

Are you dead?

No right?

So why the hell are you fighting for the dead?

Did God – Good God give you hell?

No right?

So why are you fighting to get to hell?

Good God gave you an abundance of resources now tell me, who is benefiting from the resources Good God has and have given you?

Look at Africa today and tell me, why are we not helping each other in a positive and good way?

Why are we giving our children guns to kill each other?

WHY ARE WE FIGHTING WHEN WE KNOW THAT WHEN WE FIGHT AND KILL SOMEONE OUR SPIRIT AND OR SOUL GO STRAIGHT TO HELL TO FACE JUDGEMENT THEN EVENTUAL DEATH?

So tell me now, who has the blade and who has the handle? Satan or You?

And don't you dare go there because NO AFRICAN WHETHER DEAD OR ALIVE CAN JUSTIFY RELIGION BECAUSE GOOD GOD GAVE US NONE TO DIE BY OR LIVE BY.

TRULY TELL ME, WHY ARE YOU ALLOWING WESTERN CULTURES AND CIVILIZATIONS TO DEPICT YOU, YOUR LAND AND CHILDREN AS STARVING DOGS BEGGING FOR A HANDOUT?

Truly look at the pictures of the West and tell me WHY GOOD GOD SHOULD NOT HOLD HIS HEAD DOWN IN SHAME AND DISGRACE BECAUSE OF YOU AND ALL THE EVILS YOU HAVE DONE?

TELL ME WHY GOOD GOD SHOULD NOT BE ASHAMED AT THE BLACK RACE WHEN HE LOOK UPON US?

You sold out your own, now look at Africa on a whole. Depicted like starving dogs begging at the table of their colonial masters.

Africa shouldn't have been colonized by anyone because Good God did not make us slaves, he made us like him. He made us true kings and queens that had true sight to see. But like fools we gave that up to becomes slaves to everyone including our own.

HENCE SKIN COLOUR MEANS CRAP IN THE EYES OF GOD – GOOD GOD BECAUSE IT DECAYS. MEANING WORMS EAT THE FLESH AND LEAVES THE BONES.

Our body stink – give off foul odour, so tell me how can any of us say we are pure when we stink – are foul all around? Yes hence we pass shit and say shit – tell lies.

No one wants to hear the truth but it matters to me not because like I've said, the harvest comes and every man woman and child must pay according to their works – deeds.

So Africa, I suggest you smarten up. You say you are Africans. Then represent Good God properly. He did make good and true life in your land hence true and good life came out of Africa. Good God truly loves you but you have to truly love him back.

It's amazing how we give up our own for the Babylonian way and no matter how Good God have and has shown you your faith, you still disobey him. You refuse to walk away from Babylonian injustice hence Africa has become Corrupt, Poor in History, Heritage, Black Pride, Culture, Land, Wealth, GOOD LIFE.

How the hell can any of you say you are Africans – Nubians when you know not your true history?

YOU BELONG WITH GOOD GOD BECAUSE THAT IS YOUR PLACE. GOOD GOD IS YOUR RIGHT BUT YET YOU GAVE HIM UP FOR THE DEVIL'S OWN.

Good God blessed Africa and is still blessing Africa – Nubia, but Nubia keep refusing God.

STEP AWAY FROM BABYLON BECAUSE BABYLON HAS NOR DOES BABYLON HAVE ANYTHING TO DO WITH GOD – GOOD GOD. Africa was once a great land because Good God walked the land long before the creation of Evening and you know this, so what went wrong?

I know what went wrong but do you?

GOOD GOD NEVER GAVE YOU THE RELIGIONS OF THE BABYLONIANS TO DEFILE YOURSELF INCLUDING HIM GOOD GOD AND LAND. BUT YET EACH AND EVERY DAY YOU LIVE IN YOUR CORRUPT WAY.

**Now the Aryan Nation wants you to defile your land by introducing GMO food. Trust me the day you do this Africa – Nubia can kiss Good God goodbye because you too will become extinct. Like I've said, you are Africans – Nubians and no Aryan should come into Africa and tell you how to live.**

No one should come into Nubian Land and tell you how to farm, run your country or steal your land and resources then leave you penniless in the process.

No one should come into Nubia – Africa and defile it with their germs of lies and deceit including deceitful books like the so – called holy bible.

What are you truly telling Good God? Come on now. IF YOU WERE TRUE AFRICANS – NUBIANS YOU WOULD TRULY KNOW YOUR PLACE WITH GOOD GOD AND NOT DEFILE SELF and GOD.

19

Look at Africa today without self pride and self respect. Everyone can come into your land and rape you of your self pride and dignity and you are all okay with this.

<u>Nubia was the hub to all life forms and now look at the hub. People showing you living worse than dogs begging for their nasty and dirty handouts.</u>

People can call you monkeys and coons and you're okay with that.

HENCE I ASK YET AGAIN.

WHERE IS OUR BLACK PRIDE?
WHERE IS OUR DIGNITY AND SELF RESPECT?
WHERE IS THE GOOD GOD IN ALL OF YOU?

As blacks we make Good God and our ancestors hold their heads down in shame and disgrace for what we have become literally.

Instead of living like the true Kings and Queens Good God made us to be, we live like dogs begging for bread at our slave master's table. Once again, for you Black White folks, meaning you Whites that fall under the banner of black you are included in all of this. I will go back to the Garden of Eden because like I've told you, Blacks were not the only one in the Garden of Eden for which we call Zion. Yes people in the KINGDOM OF LIONS, LYON, LYONS. Hence Good God is the female lion that protects her family in the physical and the male lion that protects his family in the spiritual realm. God's children cannot escape Zion because Allelujah is in our blood and we know how to use the Allelujah.

We know how to call on Allelujah because Allelujah is our final decree of goodness and destruction including Salvation. This is why you have the Salvation Army. Not to be confused with the Salvation Army of man but the Army meaning people of God. God's Salvation Army are his people that he truly loves and protect and if you want to exclude yourself out of this then so be it. In the end you cannot blame God for you ending up in hell. You did not heed his calling and by you ignoring his calling then you are ignoring him.

Hence I come to you the younger generation. God did not tell any of us that you can find him in a church or unholy places. Yes for some of you religion was forced down your throats but your parents, grandparents, aunts, uncles, friends and even strangers will be punished severely for this. And no do not look at me because I refuse to force anything down anyone's throat. You have two choices. Either you truly accept me or you truly reject me. When you do so you will be rejecting Good God also because like I said, he commissioned me to write him a book not once but twice. He Good God cannot say he did not because he did. Trust me, no I will not go there because Good God cannot lie even though I accuse him of lying sometimes.

YOU AS THE YOUNGER GENERATION MUST LISTEN TO GOOD COUNCIL. YOU CAN NO LONGER PARTICIPATE IN EVIL AND THINK THAT YOU ARE GOING TO BE OKAY WHEN YOU'RE NOT.

Like I've said, we are responsible for our sins. If you don't take care of self no one is going to take care of you if that person is not ordained to by God.

Being a government official or Pastor does not mean you are not responsible for your people. You are responsible for them because you signed on to take care of them. Whether you send your people to hell or not you are responsible for them. This I know now and I've said it before. As a President or Prime Minister you are responsible for the people of your land as well as the country that they live in. If you send your people to wage war against another man's land then you will be held accountable for the deaths of your people – soldiers as well as the deaths of the next man's land. *TRUST ME I SO DO NOT WANT TO BE ANY OF YOU IN HELL BECAUSE YOU HAVE TO ACCOUNT FOR THE LIVES OF THE SOLDIERS LOST AND ABSOLUTELY NOTHING YOU SAY OR DO CAN JUSTIFY YOU BECAUSE YOU WILL SEE AND HEAR:*

"THOU SHALT NOT KILL."

"THOU SHALT NOT COVET THY NEIGHBOURS WIFE." (This is the same as coveting land because you kill your neighbour for his land and or resources.)

"YOU SHALT LOVE THY NEIGHBOUR AS YOU LOVE THYSELF." (This is if your neighbour is good and true to you and Good God. If they are not, you are to separate from them. Psalms One.)

You cannot willingly kill and think all is going to be okay because it is not. Spiritual warfare is deadlier than physical warfare because it's your life – spirit that will feel this harsh pain.

Know that once war is ordained in the spiritual realm it must come to earth. It is humans that are going to feel the pain. Hence I do not know if the spaceships firing on humans represent a meteor shower that is on its way to earth.

Trust me if you think you are depressed now wait until you truly get to the spiritual realm. You know nothing about depression and spiritual pain. Hence I tell you, do not wait until you get to the grave to hear the truth because you will literally hear, "too late."

Evil hath power and I've told you this. Hence it's evil that runs earth but evil's time is up and now the harvest comes. Lands will be left barren and without food and water hence I get down on Africa to know who her people is because at the end of the day, Good God made humanity a little bit like you.

I've told you God – Good God is female in the living – physical world and male in the spiritual world. Hence we say He and this cannot change to suit anyone.

It's time we as black people wake up and start living true good and clean. If we are not living true good and clean we are living as the dead and we will go to hell and die. This I know because I've told you "HELL IS FULL OF BLACK PEOPLE." So if you are there good luck in getting out because I will not use THE KEY OF LIFE TO GET ANYONE OUT. You were the ones that chose not to listen, so suffer the consequences and feel the pain. You wanted it, so have it, it's yours.

If we are not living true good and clean we are living as dogs begging at our master's feet and table.

Life isn't about death and buying death, it's about goodness and truth including clean life.

I've told you; don't wait until you get to the grave to find out the truth. Know the truth in the living because if you find out the truth in the grave you will be too late and for billions they are too late.

I've told you before; if you are converted to Islam and you are good you are the ones that are questioned in the grave. I've yet to see any Christian being questioned in the grave. They believe in death as well as go to the houses of death and pay death to take their lives to hell with him. You sin daily and say you do not sin but you do sin. You go to whore houses and give death's children your hard earned money to die.

You believe them when they say, if you don't give 10 percent or 1/10th of your earnings you are robbing God?

Now the question I ask each and every one of you again is; how can you rob God?

Do you go into God's bank account and take his money?

Did God work for your money or did you?

You did. So how are you robbing God?

Are not your preachers robbing you and God?

Don't say no. They are robbing you and God. They are robbing you of your hard earned money and they are robbing God of you – your soul and or spirit. So who's the thief now?

What does God need your money for? Yes I've asked this before.

No come on and tell me. What does God need your money for?

Does God need it to buy clothes?
Does he need it to build his own empire?
Does he need it to buy food for his people including messengers?

Does he need the money to buy a house?

Does he need the money to buy a new car?

Now tell me this, what bank account does God have?

Can we go to God and get a loan from him?

Do these pastors even put the money they collect from you in God's bank account?

If so, where can I lodge my money in God's bank account? I know this one is an open question people. And for some strange reason I feel someone is going to come along and say, God's bank account number is this for you to deposit your hard earned money in their account. *GOD DOES NOT HAVE A BANK ACCOUNT IN MAN'S BANK. HE HAS HIS OWN HENCE HE DOES NOT REQUIRE YOU TO GIVE 1/10 OR TEN PERCENT OF YOUR WAGES.*

ALL GOD – GOOD GOD REQUIRES OF YOU IS FOR YOU TO THANK HIM FOR THE GOODNESS HE HAS AND HAVE GIVEN TO ME AND YOU.

The thieves of Satan's churches and synagogues want your

**money. Good God would never ever, infinitely never ever tell you or anyone to give him 1/10th of your earnings. Infinitely and indefinitely impossible because God is infinitely and indefinitely not a Gold Digger nor is he a BROKE NIGGA.**

SATAN IS THE BROKE NIGGA hence he has you feeding him 1/10th of your wealth. Hence the Abrahamic Code of death which falls under Melchesidec's laws of the dead – death.

Yes, _"no weapon formed against me shall prosper. God will do what he said he would do, he will stand by his word, he will come through." Excerpt from Fred Hammond's No Weapon._

Yes the spiritual war is coming and woe be unto man. Although I see all whites being massacred, I know some blacks are in this massacring. Like I've said, when evil dies – meaning wicked and evil people die, they die as white, dressed in white. So woo Nelly to the lots of you in the spiritual world because *DEATH IS SO WAITING TO PAY THE LOTS OF YOU FOR YOUR SINS. YES DEATH IS WAITING PATIENTLY TO COLLECT HIS PAY.*

What you all thought that death was done – finished?

Oh wait I forgot your book of sin told you that evil hath no power. Evil cannot harm you. When you are dead you are dead but then again evil lives by lies and feed off lies. Evil will tell you anything to keep you satisfied and this is what he has and have done.

Know this evil runs this earth.

Evil dictates to you how to worship and serve him.

Evil tells you how much money he needs every week from you and you give it to him.

Evil tells you whom to marry and you listen to him.

Evil tells you, you must die to get to him and you die to get to him – sin. (*No one can die to see Good God or God people. You die to see sin and death well your sins and your death – eventual death.*)

Evil tells you to sacrifice your child and you sacrifice your child.

Evil tells you to have sex one way and you listen to him and have sex one way.

Evil tells you to dress a certain way you listen to him.

Evil tells you he's God and you listen to him.

Evil tells you to trample down Good God and you listen to him and wear your dirty shoes in whore houses and trample down Good God and God.

Evil tells you to live a certain way you listen to him.

All that evil give us and tell us to do, we do because we want to be a part of his evil and deceitful organizations – empires. In all evil did he did not tell you, he was a giver backer taker. He did not tell you all that he gave unto you death must take you because you did sin.

THE WAGES OF SIN IS DEATH.

We all know this but we follow sin to our deaths, the death of flesh and the death of spirit.

The spiritual world does not mess around because it does affect the physical world.

I've told you war just don't happen like that in the physical world.

Death doesn't happen just like that in the physical world. So when someone tells me death hath no power, I look at them as ignorant and stupid. Many of us as black people know that man – evil and wicked people can command the dead to do their will.

Many of us black people know about Voodoo and Obeah and do participate in it, so how can any of you say the dead hath no power?

Many of us say it's an African thing because Voodoo is a religion for some. Yes it is hence the wickedness of man in the different societies of the dead. Some societies are more powerful than some but at the end of the day, they do the work of the dead – evil.

Duppy Art is real hence the practice of Voodoo and Obeah by many black people. This practice is not of God – Good God hence those who call upon the dead and use the dead including wicked and evil demons in their occult have nor has any place with Good God. Hell is there home and to hell they must and will go because they willingly hurt others for gain – financial gain – profit.

Everyone wants to get somewhere but no one is willing to go the right way to get somewhere. We would rather do wrong rather than do right. When the wrong doesn't work out we cry bodily hell and murder and say the person was not fair. They cheated you or enslaved you.

KNOW THIS: IF YOU DO NOT OPEN THE DOOR FOR EVIL TO COME IN, EVIL WOULD NOT COME IN. NOR CAN EVIL COME IN. EVIL CANNOT COME INTO WHERE IT IS NOT INVITED.

It only takes one to invite evil in and then he/she does whatever it takes to destroy it all and this is what's happening today.

Heaven and Hell is real because they are both the same from my perspective. Confusion and evil resides in the spiritual realm hence spirituality is not easily explained. The spiritual realm masks death and confuse you at times hence I do not like to translate dreams of a certain nature. I've told you, I do not want or need to decipher wrong.

Like I've said, 1313 which I say is 2013 is the end of all evil empire. 2032 but it is not 2032 but before 2032 will be the harvest – the brutal harvest of all wicked and evil empires including man. Many lands will be left barren and desolate and I've told you this. 2132 we've lost hence the destruction of humanity is before 2032. Death must provide a home for its people and for me to see the spaceships aligned and opening fire on White People then I can safely say that man, wicked and evil people are doomed. Meaning death is going to kill his own people very shortly.

No don't go there because I've told you death cannot provide food or water for his people, he can only provide or give death.

Death is not life, so death cannot give you what it can't and that's life.

There are no but buts about this because I've told you God and or Good God cannot forgive sins that were not made against him. He cannot forgive you for the sins you've done to the next man. That person must forgive you. Hence God – Good God cannot forgive you of YOUR TRESPASSES.

But what if I ask for forgiveness and he or she does not forgive me? You are probably saying.

Your asking for forgiveness goes for something as long as you are genuine honest and true in the asking. If you are not genuine honest and true, then your asking would not be looked upon or at because you were insincere – dishonest.

That person does not have to forgive you know this but do not be discouraged because you did ask truthfully. Remember that person is hurt and hurt and pain last a lifetime.

Hurt and pain is hard to let go of and forgive.

When we forget the happy times with someone, we do not forget the pain and hurt because we do not know how to truly let go of them. We do not know how to move on from that hurt hence many of us lash out and even kill. *You the person that did the hurting will have hell to pay hence the consequences of our sins is death.* I can't get around this and you can't get around this. When we sin we die. *No one can die for my sins because my sins do not go on his or her docket, it goes on mine.*

Spiritual warfare or thwarting is not nice because it does affect your physical body.

It is stress induced and if you are not careful you will die.

Remember, death knows you hence physical death is not what death is worried about but spiritual death.

SPIRITUAL DEATH IS THE FINAL DEATH.

THERE IS NO AFTER LIFE IN THE SPIRITUAL WORLD.

If your name is on death's docket then you are going to die. This is the infinite truth. You cannot change your faith in the grave. You cannot change death's docket in the grave. Once the spirit leaves the flesh truly woe be unto you if you are not good.

Once you are dead and your spirit goes down to hell then death is fine because you pose no threat to death and sin.

As a person sin allows you as a person to sin all you want because the more we sin is the further God gets from us.

Sin cannot allow you to sin in the spiritual realm because his realm is wickeder than the realm of earth. ***SIN MUST MAKE YOU SIN ON EARTH AND THIS IS WHAT HE HAS AND HAVE DONE.*** *He gives you all you want here on earth to trap you then he lets death swoop in and kill you. This is how sin works hence the "WAGES OF SIN IS DEATH."*

The more we sin is the more death has us and the more death keep us on his docket.

This phase is hard especially if you are on the right path with God. Evil does not want you to succeed so he will do all in his power to keep you from succeeding. I know this first hand. Trust me after a while you want to give up if you are the only one on the pathway or road of God – Good God. Your ideals are radical because you see the right way but have no backative.

You have no one in your corner to help you, meaning give you strength on the days you are weak. Yes I get songs and many dreams but like I've said, at times you want that human feel – touch.

The spiritual is no different from earth because your physical signature you keep. You do not lose your earthly signature meaning hue and or body. The only thing that is gone is the flesh and bones. You spirit lives on and woe be unto you in the spiritual realm.

Lord have mercy! Allelujah dear God woe be unto you. If you think you feel pain on earth now, wait until you get to the spiritual realm. You know not pain hence I tell you death mask death because he does not want to lose his spoil – you.

Trust me you don't know. You truly do not know. Oh God you truly do not know what awaits you in hell. If you are Muslim, wow, because you are going to be bound in hell. I've told you Islam is a spiritual prison and you are the ones that are bound in hell. It means there will be no escape for you. You are bound in hell for all eternity until your spirit dies. You will go through the pain and suffering of hell. No one will save you because you were born a Muslim and died a Muslim. I've told you the only ones to get the life line are those good Muslims that were converted. If they cannot answer correctly then they will be bound with the rest of the Babylonian population forever ever. Babylon introduced you to Christianity – Christos and Islam. So because you accepted them and believe them over Good God, you must go down in hell with them because they are the ones you chose.

You followed their lies to a T and because of this *EVERY MUSLIM ACROSS THE GLOBE MUST GO DOWN TO HELL AND DIE.* There are no ands ifs or buts about this. This is your life and reality and like I said, if you don't take care of it then you are lost. You will die.

The spiritual realm is not easily explained if you know nothing about it because this world is not what it seems.

Technology beyond the thought and scope of man exist in this world.

Knowledge beyond the thought and scope of man exist in this world.

Salvation is another thing hence I cannot tell you about salvation.

Yes some of you want to change from your evil ways so do it. Like I said, Psalms One is the Psalms we are to live by. I've told you this. There are no ands ifs or buts about this psalm. ***Many things we can do to save ourselves but you are the one that have to move towards that goodness and truth.***

I've raped and I've killed you are saying. All I can tell you is talk to God – Good God directly. I cannot intercede for you nor will I intercede for you. No. It's not because of what you did. I can only and talk and or speak for the people – seeds Good God has and have given me. I am truly responsible for them because Good God gave them to me.

Also, I need to grow good and true seeds and if you are not good and true then you are not for God – Good God. ***I know I have not answered you, but I don't know if I can.*** I truly do not know hence I say do not give up on Good God. If your goodness that you do now cannot go for you, let it go for your children – your family and the family you've hurt. If this is what you honestly want to do tell God – Good

God because we've all sinned in our life and a sin is a sin. We die. *If we sin not we do not die but as long as we continue to sin we will die in the physical and spiritual world.*

And no, it's never too late to do an ounce of good. Remember tomorrow comes and it is given. Tomorrow just turn into today. We see tomorrow today. These two are no different. Humanity just confuse you when it comes to tomorrow because they know not about tomorrow. They only know today. Tomorrow for you maybe the next day, but tomorrow for God and Good God can be three months from now or even 9 months. Hence I've told you spiritual time is not the same as physical time. I've told you spiritual time is further ahead in time and it is physical time to reach that point in time where it catches up to spiritual time.

All these things you should know by now hence I tell you spiritual time – the spiritual is hard for me to explain if you know nothing about it.

Evil is real and it does exist.

Yes you have people that are ordained by Good God to break every evil spell imaginable to man. And people do not look at me. Like I said, do not give me Names and labels because I will get angry. I am doing what was required of me and I chose and choose to write and teach truth. If you hate me for this, then you have a problem.

We as human beings have and has strayed and now the spaceships in the spiritual realm is aligned to kill just like the picture on the first page. The only difference is, the spaceships were greater in numbers.

We caused this because we are the ones to sin big time whilst forgetting that the wages of sin is death.

We are the ones to sin daily.
We are the ones to ignore life.

The deed is done hence the spiritual war comes to earth. Woe be unto man this time around because this realm is going to pour out your sorrows on you. No not its sorrows but your sorrows. Your sins did down to death and death must collect his pay.

So truly woe be unto us because it is going to be deadly for humanity. The harvest has and have been commissioned. Humanity must now catch up to that time in time and when we do reach that time, billions are going to die. We are going to feel it because we kill and take without remorse.

We kill for sport hence we take lives.

We kill but yet cannot give life nor can we create life.

We tell lies to others without knowing that in the end we are going to die.

Right now all that surrounds us is death because we do sin and we do tell lies.

Death is our cry hence Babylon's kingdom must fall. It must go down to hell never to rise again.

So in all that is said, the Aryan nation must go down because the true Aryans of old from my dream are Spaniards. Many hate black people and if they could wipe us off the face of the planet they would, hence many believe in Christos – White Death.

The fighting in the spiritual world will not stop because the planet of sin was given power by man – humanity.

We are the sinful ones that are governed by sin in the physical and the spiritual. Hence shortly, many lands will become barren – a total wasteland.

Africa, Africa I am crying out to you.
Save your land
Do not give the enemies a home

Do not let them flee to you
Do not let them continue to destroy you

Africa is on the docket of the wicked
Do not let them conquer you
DO NOT LET THEM ENSLAVE YOU AGAIN
DO NOT SELL OUT YOUR PEOPLE AGAIN

Look at Africa – Nubia
Truly look at her and relish in her beauty
Wisdom is yours
The kingdom of God – Good God is truly yours

Reclaim it
Walk in African Pride

You are the pride and joy of our ancestors
You are hope for a better tomorrow

Tomorrow does come because everything surrounds
tomorrow including Yesterday – You

Today is tomorrow because tomorrow turns into
today and today turn into yesterday.

Ah Mama Africa, many of Good God's children want
to come home. Receive us in goodness and kindness.
Truly know us because truth must return to Nubia
and we must reclaim our heritage for us to move on.

Mama Africa, we have to come back and build you in a positive way.

We must build you in a positive way.

Mama, Mama Africa, we truly want to come home to you.

Truly receive Good God's good children and let us raise you up to see him (Good God).

Let us truly build you in truth and harmony.

Let us go up in pride and joy to Good God forever ever forevermore.

Michelle Jean

The door is open because little by little everything is being revealed.

Humanity will know the truth because nothing can stop the truth. The spiritual world is just like the physical world because death hath power. Hence it is death that takes your spirit from the flesh.

Death cannot kill the spirit just like that because every man that hath sin on their record must pay. They must taste hell before his or her eventual death.

So when a man say the bible say, the dead hath no power. Say to them, the dead hath power because it is the dead as well as death that takes all human life whether physical or spiritual. Hence death has power. The dead hath power because the dead – evil dead does torment you. Humans have no power over death if he or she is not ordained by Good God to do so.

Many things happen in the spiritual that humans know nothing about, hence I've told you spiritual technology is far more advanced than human technology. Things that we cannot solve are solved in the spiritual realm. The information then flows down to man meaning are given to man in the forms of dreams, writings, songs and sightings amongst other things.

The spiritual world is simple but yet complex. Good is fueled by good in the spiritual world and sins are fueled by sins hence the planet of evil or the planet where evil comes from. Yes the planet of death.

Evil has a greater following on earth and it is because of these enormous sins that we do on a daily basis earth is going to be destroyed. The wicked of earth are the ones to be destroyed hence I've told you about the harvest that is coming and woe be unto man. Our sins created this deadly harvest hence we cannot blame anyone but self.

Africa I am coming to you.

AFRICA DO NOT DAM UP YOUR WATERWAYS BECAUSE YOU ARE GOING TO NEED IT. GOOD GOD GAVE AFRICA AN ABUNDANCE OF WATER AND OIL FOR A REASON AND THE REASON IS AND WILL ALWAYS BE TO PREPARE FOR THE HARVEST THAT IS COMING.

Your land will now feed Western and Eastern civilizations. ***YOU WILL RISE AGAIN AND NO ONE CAN STOP THIS RISE.***

AFRICA IS FOR AFRICANS. HENCE I TELL YOU KNOW WHO YOUR PEOPLE ARE BECAUSE NOT

EVERYONE IS OF GOOD GOD OR OF NUBIA – AFRICA.

Africa is the mother ship and flag ship of the universe and you cannot continue to disgrace Good God with your fighting and bickering including corruption. Good God did not make us sinful we made ourselves sinful.

We deceived self by believing in the lies of the Babylonians.

We have to stop this now. Come on now.

Listen, I am truly tired of everyone using Africa and you as Africans not seeing it. Take care of your own because as it is right now, the West and Eastern countries want to finish what they started. If you let them do this, then you are telling God and Good God that Nubia and her children were not worth it in the first place.

NOW I AM GOING TO BE RACIST HERE BECAUSE I WENT ON A TWITTER RANT THIS MORNING (NOVEMBER 10TH 2013). I don't care if Twitter bans me for using the f word. But I am fucking tired of people degrading Africa when it was the black race and black race alone created this universe. No other race created it. We created all life forms including the given races hence every human being have a trace of

46

black in them. Your scientists today use some bullshit like DNA to say otherwise, hence they try to manipulate the genes with chemicals, genetically modified foods that kills you slowly. They want a world that is man made to say God – Good God did not create the world or universe. But they will never have it hence the harvest comes. NO ONE CAN DISPROVE GOD – GOOD GOD. NO ONE BECAUSE HUMANITY KNOWS NOT GOD – GOOD GOD NOR DO THEY KNOW GOODNESS. ALL HUMANS KNOW IS EVIL HENCE FOR BILLIONS DEATH WILL BE THEIR HOME – FINAL DEATH.

And no that was not the racist rant this is.

I finally got twitter and I want to close it down because certain things I can't deal with. So to the Babylonian that said, he has half his beer left to drink and that he has to drink it because people are starving in Africa. Go fuck yourself and fuck off Mfucker. Africans – the black race are spiritual beings that let your cave dwelling, incest practicers into our abode via Eve. You're all fing family rams that like to fuck each other so don't fucking pass your place.

Africa is not broke. Africa just let the wrong people in and they raped us of our lands, heritage, wealth, beauty, pride, spirituality, freedom, culture, peace, language, dignity, women and men including Good God himself.

We were never slaves. We were Kings and Queens long before you knew about Kings and Queens. We did not sleep with family members but you did. We learnt this nastiness from your nasty breed. Hence the world is riddled with sin because humans follow and worship your stinking nasty and degenerate gods.

Don't class Africans like you because we do not wallow in filth and not all of us bow down to your cesspool of gods that take you straight to hell.

DULY NOTE AND REMEMBER, AFRICA – NUBIA NEVER STOLE FROM YOU OR ANYONE. EVERY NATION ON THE FACE OF THIS PLANET STOLE FROM AFRICA – NUBIA. SO DON'T FUCKING PASS YOUR PLACE BECAUSE MANY OF US DO NOT WANT ANYTHING FROM YOU CONNIVING AND DECEITFUL RACE. SO FUCK YOU AND TAKE YOUR PASS STRAIGHT TO HELL BITCH.

Damn wrenk. No wonder none of you are the mountain of Good God because truth is *YOU'RE ALL SATAN'S SEED.* Go back to Genesis of your book of sin bitch and read what it said. Good God did not put enmity between his seed and Satan's seed. Enmity was already there. *You're all fucking jealous of black* _**people because Good God favours us over your conniving and deceitful ass**. Despite our sinful ways he's been looking out for us and helping us but we are the ones to ignore him._ And any White person step to me and say I am a racist bitch I will put you on blast big time.

I AM INFINITELY TRULY SICK OF EVERYONE DEGRADING AFRICA AND AFIRCANS LIKE WE ARE NOT HUMANS.

Whites hate blacks

Chinese hate blacks

Babylonians hate blacks – yes Indians for all that is going to say she did not say Indians.

Black hate blacks

Satan hates black – no he just deceived Eve.

What have the black race done unto you for every nation including their own hating on them as well as hate them.

To jump ahead of myself. November 15, 2013 I saw this twitter image. I went on the Africa site and this thing put up a picture of underage black boys that was so disgusting it made me sick. The picture had one child laying on the ground with sperm on him and the other boys ejaculating on him. Meaning they ejaculated on him and this creep had the nerve to say, *"this is what they doing in Africa nah I'll keep my 5 cents a day."* These are underage children and he made a comment like that. I went on a twitter rant because it is obvious to me that these minors are being used in the sex trade.

I was so hurt that I sent out direct messages to a few people to see if they can do something. Two people direct messaged me back, so hopefully they can help because no one should see children in a manner like that.

The creep that posted the picture retweeted one of my tweets but had the nerve to say bitch I can buy you or something of the sort. Man did I ever cuss him. "You can buy me."

IS THIS WHAT BLACK PEOPLE HAVE AND HAS BECOME FOR A STINKING PIECE OF DECOMPOSED MEAT TO TELL ANOTHER HUMAN BEING. THEY CAN BUY THEM.

Yes I am mad hence my harsh words above. To me, he condones this nastiness hence his comment to me and my rant in this book.

Our children are being sexually abused and used and humanity is okay with this. No wonder hell is there.

And yes out of anger I commissioned his ass to hell literally. I told him to burn in hell hence he has no part or parcel including place with Good God. He is done. This includes his family. Yes I feel sad to commission him to hell in my anger and I told Good God about it but my mind kept telling me not to have any remorse. Right now I don't because kids are being hurt and instead of him helping, he did nothing. He can make his nasty remarks and say he can buy me.

Well buy hell now because I just commissioned you to hell with your family. See how it feels in hell now.

No one should hurt a child or see injustice being done to children – innocent children and do nothing about it. I don't give a shit what your nationality is.

Being BLACK does not make me any different from you.

We are the same in life and death hence the color of human skin is not valued because both skin color represent the different stages and type of death.

You cannot condone nastiness like this hence I am signing off twitter because they condone nastiness like this.

Just as I've turned off Facebook because of half naked pictures, I am turning off twitter. Don't need to see garbage like this nor do I need to see half naked selfies. The people of earth is done because not one of us have pride in self nor do we have any self respect.

BLACK PEOPLE IT'S TIME WE WAKE UP AND STOP DISGRACING SELF AND START RESPECTING SELF.

We created it all now look at how we are depicted and classed.

Where is our self respect?

We were the creators now we are classed and valued less than dogs and we are okay with this? Come on now.

Oh my head because it is hurting me. God – Good God, is this what you want for the black race?

Put aside everything because I am now talking about colour of skin now.

Everyone has and have raped us of our self respect, our heritage, our beauty, our pride, and you and you are okay with this?

Truly look at what other nations have done to Africa.

Truly look at what we as blacks have done to self and Africa and tell me if you do no hold your head down in shame and disgrace to see what your children have and has become to others?

Nothing that you can say to me can or will justify you or what your true people have to go through at the hands of wicked and vile people – demons.

Many things I will forgive you for but I truly don't think I can forgive you for what the Black Race have been put through.

I know our past present and future life, but is this what you truly wanted for us?

We have been raped and robbed of everything including our self respect and dignity and you want us to continue this way? If so, then I say to you, you are not fair and you are unjust.

If this is what you want for our people as well as your chosen few, then I have to truly walk away from you.

You are not true nor are you good and holy, peaceful – true love if this injustice is what you want for your own black people.

We have no morals anymore hence Sodom and Gomorrah is global. The nastiness and vileness of these lands has and have come to life in what we call the modern and global world of this day and time. Every country on the face of this planet can call themselves Sodom and Gomorrah because of the lawlessness and lack of morals that is been spread in the entertainment world as well as in the home.

 Yes I've brought colour into this on one level. And no I will not remind anyone of the BLACK BANNED because I am tired of explaining it. Anyone that do not like what I write can chuck the middle finger and blow. Yes I am capable of racism and I tell you when I am being racist. If I don't it's an oversight on my part so truly forgive me. There are no distinction in colour of skin and I will repeat, *"GOOD GOD DOES NOT REFUSE ANYONE FROM HIS KINGDOM BASED ON RACE. HE DOES REFUSE YOU BASED ON THE LIES YOU TELL AND SINS THAT YOU COMMIT."*

And yes lies are sins.

Right is right and wrong is wrong and I am tired of the African Stereotypes hence sometimes you have to put some people in their damned place. Yes Good God

**I overstepped my boundaries this morning but I refuse to make an apologies because there is none to be made.** Like I said, I am a defender and I will defend my people which are your people.

It's time for Africans to wake up Good God because you did give us that land and no one has a right to come in and create war and strife amongst us. Every African across the globe can say Africa – Nubia belongs to them. No other race can say this because you gave Africa Life, meaning Life Started in Africa and branched out. Europeans claim Europe and that is their right but they cannot claim Africa because no Europeans lived there. Zion (Lion) is different from earth because Zion (Lion) is a holy place, meaning no sin can enter there. It is clean and pure, void of all sin and sinful beings – spirit. We the black race know this hence we sing about it. Songs are important to you Good God hence we carry on the tradition of knowledge – speech. When our writings were taken from us by our slave masters we had to resort to singing, dancing, drumming, prayers, chants and more to tell our story. What to find other means of communication to tell what was happening to us and we did. Hence we carry on tradition of truth but our tradition became distorted and diluted when we accepted the Babylonians into our land. They polluted our lands hence we became dirty as well as lost our true sight to tell time and what was going to happen in time. We lost our spirituality including you Good God like I've said.

Many things we did but yet the world class us so low.

We are classed lower than dogs and instead of the black race waking up and moving back to Africa to build Africa in a positive and good way, we let others go into the land and destroy it.

We build other lands instead of building our true ancestral home.

We build self and destroy self instead of using some of our wealth to help build Africa.

Many lands are now rejecting us, so tell me Good God, what is the black man truly going to do when the harvest comes? I know and you know many will be overlooked by the system because they have no part in the new system the devil is trying to implement.

We allow the devil to give us religion and steal us now look at us? Like beggars – swines in pig pens waiting for the slop of their masters.

We let others go into Africa – Nubia and give us filth – garbage called religion – Christianity and Islam amongst other stinking religions and say it is good for us.

RELIGION IS PORK, UNCLEAN MEAT THAT DEFILES GOD – GOOD GOD AND YOU.

He Good God never gave us religion to defile self.

Evil gave us his filth and we accept it. Now look at humanity today. **Following the book of sin that teaches us it's okay to kill and wallow in incest.**

This is the nastiness that sin – wicked and sinful people teach us and we say it is of God – Good God.

No wonder we are lost and truly locked out of Good God's kingdom.

How can incest be of God – Good God when incest is a sin?

It is a sin for family members to lay with family members. We all know this but yet we say God – Good God condones this.

It is a sin for a grown ass man to lay with a children and we all know this but yet we condone it because rapists and pedophiles in the church say it is of God and you believe them.

This is a child – our children and we freely and willingly give them over to sin. Wicked and evil men and women to rape them. Have sex with them hence screwing up their future and psychological well being. Well to the lots of you that willingly do this, hell is waiting because there is a special place in hell that is reserved for you this I guarantee. Trust me infinitely on that because I am trusting death – the father of death to make your hell hotter than that of death. This I request of God – Good God to carry out meaning let the father of death add to his list of things to do if it is possible.

We knowingly hurt our children for what?

They did not ask to come into this world. Yes I complain about mine but I would not knowingly hurt them or hand them over to stranger to use and abuse them. And yes I know it's not just strangers that abuse our children, family member's abuse our children also. We talk about family values but there are no family values in society today. I can't see it. I see the need for a change but I cannot change you, you have to change yourself because our children are being led astray.

This negative force and force field that surrounds earth – humanity has to stop.

Look at the young entertainers today and how they are behaving. Our children are watching them and the crap they are doing. It's gotten so bad that I rarely watch television. I don't want to see them and their whorish behaviour because they are setting no example for anyone. Nor are they setting a good example for the future generation.

We have lost our self pride and dignity.

Truly take a look at the people of the world and tell me, who is governing us because it's certainly not Good God.

We've become a nation of destructive and self destructive people and this is why the harvest comes.

Sin wasn't doing this to help humanity. SIN WAS DOING THIS TO KILL YOU and he's succeeded in doing so.

Like I've told you, I see things before me. I am going to endorse my other line of books here. If you go to Lulu.com or Google and type in Kane and Nubia you will see the cover of my book. This is how I saw the sky before me but the lightning was more severe. I don't know what this means but if you know let me know. I don't have to dream to see things and tell you things because I see things in front of me. I've not seen many ugly faces lately. I am now seeing beautiful white faces. Some smiling and some not smiling so I don't know.

So now that I have told you about blacks, I have to tell you about whites because I am seeing more white people now. More than likely I will call these books Whiteman Redemption. Once I begin to see the white side of things I will let you know. And no I am not being racist. Like I've said, there is a White Death and a Black Death and I have to give both sides whether you like it or not. *What's good for the goose is also good for the gander that's all I got to say, so lay off with your racist bullshit.* Not on my watch. *I can't talk about blacks without talking about whites.*

Yes I've gone way beyond where I wanted to go but that's just me.

Back On Board Again.

60

Like I said above, the spiritual is simple but complex. This world is not an easy realm to pinpoint because of the deciphering that must be done.

Things happen in the spiritual world hence I touched on spiritual sex a while back.

There is something called spiritual sex. It is beautiful and I am going to say magical. Spiritual sex is rare but it does happen.

PLEASE NOTE THAT SPRITUAL SEX IS NOT THE SAME AS HAVING SEX WITH A GHOST.

There are implications when you sleep with ghosts – demons. I don't want to talk about duppies or ghost because then I have to talk about dead weight and physical weight. I know some people say the spirit has no mass but the spirit has mass. The spirit can make your body as light as a feather and it can make it heavier than a tonne.

Just know that ghosts do sleep with human beings and some literally have sex with humans. That's why some of us are sick and don't know why we are sick.

Some of us die and don't know why we die. There is something called a head blow. We Jamaicans know *about head blows because some of us can see ghosts as plain as day. We can describe the person as well as the clothing the person is wearing.*

Ghosts do follow people.

Ghosts do eat food and this is why some people leave food out for the dead.

Ghosts do eat with you. Many things ghosts do that you don't know hence ghosts kill humans.

Ghosts are no different from me and you because they look like me and you. When you see the ugliness of a ghosts you are seeing that persons sins. That person's true self because of sin, the sins he or she did on earth. Hence if a Jamaican say, "YU UGLY LACKA SIN," know that you are damned ugly in the worst kind of way. And no "YU UGLY LACKA WHA," is not the same as "YU UGLY LACKA SIN". We all know sin is damned ugly.

Yes I am proud of my heritage because in my ways our heritage when all is gone, our heritage stays with us. When you can get rid of things, we cannot get rid of our heritage because our heritage is our link to our ancestors.

More importantly, OUR HERITAGE IS OUR TRUE LINK TO GOOD GOD.

No one can give back their heritage because our heritage is engrained in us. It is a part of our bloodline – DNA. It is a part of our life story not apart history or his story.

Yes I can go on, but that's if for man. Well wicked and evil men because earth must reclaim that which is hers.

Earth must rise up against man – humanity and we see this happening now with the different hurricanes and tidal waves. We treated earth like shit literally. Now it's time for us to vacate her land in the harshest of ways.

We cut down her trees
Pollute her waterways
We bury all manner of disgust in her
We even bury our dead and feces in her
We've contaminated her
Told lies in her
Did all manner of evil in her, now she wants her pay and that is with the lives of all wicked and evil people. They must come out of her because her cries have and has reached far and wide – extremely high.

She was given to us and in all she did to protect us, we destroyed her. Took from her, abused her children and kingdom. We took her for granted even spat on her. We've all done it and never one day have we said, Good God, truly thank you for Mother Earth because she did shelter us from the storm. She gave us clean water to drink and food to eat and we truly, truly thank you for her and what she has done for us.

In all that we did, we thought of self and self only. Now it's too late for man because man have and has totally destroyed her.

She cannot take the pain anymore hence she has become old and polluted, aged beyond repair. All that was to keep her is gone. Why? No one can answer because like I've said, none have truly thought about her. All we do is cut down and built. Destroy all in sight. Now look how many animals are gone off the face of this planet. Extinct, never to return thanks to the greed of man – humanity.

We have become vile in the eyes and sight of God hence, it is our vileness of sin that will kill us and take us straight to hell and burn.

When man is gone earth will slowly rebuild. Yes it will take centuries for her to rebuild and get rid of the filth of man but it must be done hence the extinction of man - humanity.

Michelle Jean

Yes it's hard I know but this is the reality of man.

Developed civilizations that rape and kill will be no more because every last morsel of food and water must be taken from them.

The earth has declared the glory of Good God and man must now vacate earth and find another home. Earth is rebelling and so man will be no more.

She should have done this a long time ago but now she is doing it. The devil's time is up and it's now time to clean house and reclaim her home – own.

Like I said, humanity love to live by lies and it is because of these lies, humanity is slated to die and I've told you this before.

Many things are going to happen. I cannot see everything but what I see, I tell you and I will not stop telling you.

Wow I would like to go off again but today I won't. I'm having weird dreams again and I know not how to decipher them.

Before I go on I have to ask this question.

WHY DO BABYLONIAN LANDS THINK THEY ARE HOLY?

Good God never gave them life – his life but yet they claim to be and they are INFINITELY AND INDEFINITELY NOT APART OF AFRICA – NUBIA.

So how can a land that is not a part of Nubia – Africa say they are holy, when they are not a part of God's plan – world?

Which land on the face of this planet is holy?

What is a holy land when death walks the land, kill on land – take at will?

What is a holy land when people write lies and tell lies on Good God in his own land?

How can you say your land is holy when your land was once a part and still is a part of the Babylonian System of death?

Yes the name changes hence the Abrahamic Law of Death that is carried out by Abraham's followers and people.

Yes I am bent but not truly bent because I know the lies of the So-Called Jews hence Revelations called them out.

I know the lies and deceit of the Israelites and Judahites hence the book of sin called them out.

I know the end of man – wicked and evil men hence the time frame of all evil is before 2032.

13 is the number that evil fairs. Well 13 has come and every wicked and evil nation including people will die. They will go down to hell and burn for the sins they have committed on land.

On to my dream

It's November 11, 2013 and the dreams are confusing.

I dreamt about blue seas and the beauty of Jamaica.

The sea was beautiful and pretty, hence I truly do not know what is going on with death and the land of my birth – Jamaica.

Jamaica I am confused hence confusion surrounds me. My dreams are confusing me as to you. Maybe there is hope for the land yet. Who knows? Hence I will leave my dreams of you this morning alone.

Okay. I dreamt I was back home and my uncle's wife and son had died. They were buried in the back of the yard. So I went to see the grave but where I went no grave was there. All I saw was a knife in the ground. The blade was in the ground and the black handle of the knife was sticking up.

I don't know who took me to the grave but the person said Mama is right there but I could not see any grave. There were lots of bushes – dead bushes on the grave and the person that was with me started to clean the bush for me to see the graves.

Cleaning the graves for me to see, I saw two green patch on the graves and pigs on the grave.

He even made the lines separating the graves. The graves were supposed to be square but I still could not see the graves. Weird because pigs – swines were on the graves and I think I saw a circular swirl but I can't remember. But I know a circular swirl was there.

This is a weird dream and if you can make sense out of it please do so because things are getting weird. I am also dreaming in the past again. I cannot tell you what I saw in the past because my mind refuses to retain the information.

I can only tell you the bits I remember. But to have pigs – swines on a grave is disturbing to me because I've never seen pigs on a grave before. Yes my uncle has a pig pen and it's by the pig pen area the graves were.

It's also the first time I am seeing a knife with the blade in the ground and the handle upright. Trust me people I am clueless with this one.

Hence I am going to tell Africa – Nubia to start planting **ORGANIC** fruit baring trees, herbs, spices, breadfruit trees, jackfruit trees, mango trees, moringa trees, cedar trees, sugarcane, yam, banana, coffee, cocoa, plantain; all that is good to eat start planting it. Like I've said, the land with the food and water will be the richest land on the face of the planet.

Good God gave Africa an abundance of land and water for a specific reason hence you are highly favored and blessed.

DO NOT SELL OFF YOUR LAND AND WATERWAYS TO FOREIGNERS.

Stop killing yourselves and start using the resources of the soil because if you let your land and waterways go to

foreigners, then BLACK PEOPLE ARE TRULY DOOMED.

Africa need its land and waterways. So to the governments of Africa, start hiring your own people to till some of the government owned land from now so that when the people in developed nations are starving, you have the resources to feed them meaning sell them your food.

EVERYONE IS FIGHTING FOR THE OIL OF THE LANDS BUT THE OIL IS GOING TO BE DRIED UP. THERE ARE NO ANDS IFS OR BUTS ABOUT THIS. IT IS GOING TO HAPPEN. SO I AM TELLING YOU TO SECURE THE FUTURE OF YOUR PEOPLE AND STOP THE FIGHTING AND START PLANTING. ABSOLUTELY NEVER EVER TURN TO GMO OR GENETICALLY MODIFIED FOODS. STAY ORGANIC BECAUSE IF YOU GO GMO THEN GOOD GOD WILL INFINITELY TURN FROM YOU.

Truly listen because all everyone do is rape Africa of her dignity and resources. Including rape us of our African pride and you cannot continue to let this happen.

God – Good God found favour in you. So turn from the Babylonian Way of doing things and start living like true Africans – Children of the Preferred. God –

Good God did choose you because it was you. (Figure it out if you can).

IF HE DIDN'T, HE WOULD NOT HAVE MADE LIFE START IN AFRICA. NOR WOULD HE HAVE JOINED LIFE IN SOUTH SUDAN.

You are a beautiful set of people with a magnificent skin tone that I truly love to look upon. I need to forever ever thank God – Good God for making me behold the beauty of his black and gorgeous people. So stop disrespecting self and hold your head up in pride.

Stop bleaching your skin to look like White Death – FINAL DEATH. Black is gorgeous hence the banner of Good God is black and this banner can infinitely never ever change to suit any given race of people.

Truly love Africa and save it.

Stop killing self and respect you – the colour Good God has and have given you.

Respect your true heritage which is the heritage of God – Good God.

PUT AWAY THE RELIGIONS OF THE BABYLONIANS AND LIVE LIFE TRUE GOOD AND CLEAN.

Good God did not give Babylonians life and you all know this.

TRUE AFRICANS DO NOT KILL THEIR OWN NOR DO THEY FIGHT FOR WHAT DOES NOT BELONG TO THEM.

TRUE AFRICANS DO NOT FOLLOW OR WALLOW IN THE NASTINESS OF THE BABYLONIANS. HENCE GOOD GOD INFINITELY NEVER EVER GAVE US THE RELIGIONS OF MEN TO DEFILE US OR HIM. NOR DID HE GIVE US RELIGIONS OF MEN TO DEFILE THE EARTH AND ALL THAT HE HAS AND HAVE CREATED.

HE GOOD GOD GAVE US SPIRITUAL KNOWLEDGE TO MAINTAIN AND SAVE US AS WELL AS HELP US IN OUR JOURNEY HERE ON EARTH.

No African can say they are of God – Good God and live like the heathens of old – the Babylonians.

Remember we were separated from the Babylonians.

Good God saw it befitting to separate us and we must stay separate and apart from them. So truly clean up Africa in a good way BECAUSE ONCE THE HARVEST STARTS AND YOU ARE NOT CLEAN WOE BE UNTO YOU AND YOUR LAND.

AFRICA YOU ARE BEING WARNED SO TRULY TAKE HEED and clean your lands up so that when the harvest fully hits you will be safe. You don't have to listen to me. Go back to Daniel of the Book of Sin and learn about the harvest from his day and time. We are no different today. We must face the harvest because as humans, we did sin vile and wicked in the eyes and sight of God – Good God.

AFRICA LISTEN TO ME AND HEAR GOOD GOD.

DO WELL AND GOOD BY YOUR LAND AND PEOPLE SO THAT WHEN DEATH SWEEPS OVER EARTH, YOUR LAND AND PEOPLE WILL BE SAFE.

Truly stop the sinning and killing and ask God – Good God for repentance. Repent of your sins and let your land and people be free from death.

The economy of the Western World and Eastern World must collapse. Not all but some. You are in a good position with land and water so clean your countries up and live.

Good God gave you life so truly take care of it because if you don't you will hear "TOO LATE."

You cannot fail God come on now.

You cannot continue to turn from God come on now.

So truly listen to Good God and live.

AFRICA IS MORE THAN WORTH IT BECAUSE GOOD GOD GAVE AFRICA ALL THAT WHICH IS GOOD FROM HIM. So truly feed yourself and the world. It is your destiny.

Michelle Jean

BACK ON COURSE

Spiritual war wow because who feels it knows it.

Know that in the spiritual world to be white does not mean you are white. I've shown you Peter Tosh was shown to me as white person. Hence you have to figure things out and you do figure it out.

Like I've said above, the white people that I saw being killed could be black people being killed but I seriously doubt this because I was an on looker.

Michelle Jean

It's a new day and I am depressed. Hence these few lines because somehow I need to be heard. These words have nothing to do with spiritual war. It's my feeling hence I am sharing them with you.

By now you know that I do not do things normally and to be honest this is the way I want and need it to be sometimes, not all the time.

HERE WE GO

Do hope you enjoy because I am deep in thought or in question for some of you.

But you are racist you are saying.

Can't help you I got to be me.

MICHELLE JEAN

ENJOY

My God My God why have thou abandoned me and my family – children?

Why have you forsaken me?

I need help all around and you've neglected me

You've shown me no mercy as of late when it comes to raising my children alone.

You've shown me no mercy in providing for me as of late.

You've shown me no mercy in raising them.

My family is a dysfunctional one. Instead of guiding me on the right path of raising them and securing their future, you've done absolutely nothing of the sort as of late.

You asked me to do a job and I am doing it but when it comes to my sanity and when it comes to raising my children the right and proper way, you are not truly there for me.

I am tired God truly tired.

Tell me something. How many more years must I wait for you to hear me?

How many more years must I wait in vain for you to be a true honest good and caring father as well as the disciplinarian I need for my children?

God I told you I cannot do it alone but here I am on this lonely road walking alone and raising my children alone. I know you are there in the background but that is no consolation to me. I need you beside me. I need you here with me in the physical and spiritual to truly help me in a good and true way.

You are father but you are not a good father to my children when it comes to taking charge of their lives and talking to them.

I can't bare the pain anymore hence I want out. I need a true vacation from you because I truly cannot depend on you to be the true father that I need for my children.

I need you but where are you when it comes to me and my children?

Where is your true love of me and my children?

Michelle Jean
November 12, 2013

God you see my pain
My hurt
My sorrow but yet you ignore me

I need you to adopt my children in a good way and for you to lead them on the right track as well as lead them on the path of goodness and truth.

I need you to lead them on the pathway of honesty and cleanliness; infinite goodness.

God – Good God, what have I done that is so displeasing in thy sight for you to be neglecting my children as well as me?

Tell me something God – Good God. Why have you dumped me by the roadside like some piece of garbage?

Why have you neglected my home and family – children like we are worth nothing in thy sight?

Why do you not look upon us in goodness and in truth?

God – Good God, why have you truly forsaken me?
Why have you truly forsaken my children?
Why have you left us to suffer and die especially me?

We need you.
I need you

In all that I have done even tried to do in goodness and in truth it counts for naught in thine eyes.

Tell me something Good God.

Did you not ask me to write you a book twice and I've been writing. So tell me, where did I go wrong with you and in all that I've written?

Why are you not helping me to raise my children the right and proper way?

Why forsake them and treat them like nothing as if they are not a part of your kingdom and good life.

Tell me what I am doing wrong as a parent and truly help me to correct my wrongs in a positive and good way.

I am depending on you but you are pushing me aside.

You are neglecting me as of late.

Please tell me why and truly help me to correct the things that I am doing wrong?

Michelle Jean
November 12, 2013

God – Good God are you the hard way in my life?
Are you the deceitful and lying one in my life?

You are God but yet I cannot take my problems to you anymore. It's as if your door is temporarily locked to me and I so do not know why.

I need help – true help and you are ignoring me.

Why?

Why do you not see me and my family – children?

It's like you want me to fail at all I do so that you can laugh at me.

You want me to fail so that you can say trusting fool.

You want me to fail for trusting you and truly loving you.

Tell me something. How can this be when it comes to me and you?

I don't know anymore God – Good God because my world is turned upside down.

My life has and have been turned down. All that I've done to rise up in a good and true way – a positive way I cannot rise. I am being shot down.

All that I've done to help me and my family including you I've failed, so I truly give up because I do not know what else to do.

I've failed life and in life because there is no rise for me.

I am bound and chained in the depths of hell.
I am confused
Burdened
Ill
This I know now hence I have to leave you alone.

My life is too hard.

One hand cannot wash Good God and you know this but yet you leave me alone to struggle and make life with one hand. I am like a one wheel cart but yet I am making do in the struggle and in some strange kind of way, I truly thank you because despite the illness of feet, I am still walking and getting from A to B.

I've been walking alone God but today I cannot walk alone anymore hence I have to come off your road temporarily because it's too damned hard for me and on me.

Michelle Jean
November 12, 2013

God – Good God you've failed me health wise
You've failed me financially
You've failed me spiritually
You've failed me family wise
You've failed me companionship wise
You've failed me all around.

Yes Good God this is the way I feel because mentally I am broken.

Spiritually I am broken

Trust wise I am broken and you refuse to fix me because I cannot fix myself. Yes I want you to because you are the best fixer of them all. Yes I am being selfish but I want to be today for some strange reason.

You refuse to aid me in my family crisis at home
You refuse to aid me all around

Yes this is how I am feeling today. I have to tell you these things because this is truly how I feel and this is the true me. You know this is you and me so truly listen and stop ignoring me.

The respect is not there when it comes to you respecting me.

The true love isn't there when it comes to you truly loving me.

I truly can't give you anymore of me because I am truly burnt out and stressed out.

Truth costs nothing Good God so why are you costing me?

Why are you taxing me health wise, mental wise, spiritual wise, physical wise, financially wise, true love wise, death wise and sin wise just to name a few?

Truly tell me Good God why you're taxing me?

Can truth tax truth?
Can true love tax true love? So why are you taxing me?

I cannot continue to give you true love and get nothing in return. And no this nothing is not something, so truly don't go there.

There is no true love there on your part when it comes to me. I cannot live on false hope anymore. I cannot live on your lies. I have a life and I have to live for truth so that I can become infinitely truthful and honest. Yes greater in truth and true love than you. Yes I went there so don't you dare say Oh is that so.

I have to truly live for me now because in all you've done, you truly don't see me nor do you remember me in your day to day going in and coming in, including your true giving of goodness and truth.

I truly need Good God but you cannot satisfy my needs.

I have to do for me now because I need true happiness in my life.

I need true peace and harmony not only in my life but in my mind body and soul – spirit.

I do not need the negative forces of hell around me anymore. I need to break free and truly be the good me that I need to be.

Good God, I rely on you for all but as of late I find I cannot rely on you for anything.

As of late we are not there for each other. Well I'm there for you but you are not truly there for me.

I truly can't do this anymore so come 2014 I am leaving you temporarily. Yes I am going on a true vacation without you.

Michelle Jean
November 12, 2013

If I had known the road of Good God was so rough, I would have never walked on it. I would have chosen another path of goodness and truth. In all He Good God asks you to do you have to do it alone. You have to bare the burdens alone.

You have to feel the pain and hardships alone.

You have to bare the loneliness alone.

You have to take the disrespect of children and others alone.

At times you feel defeated and say why me?

At times you want to give up like me and although you are told don't give up, you have to because of the pain you feel inside.

You feel abandoned by all including Good God. So you say, what's the purpose of it all when even the one you truly love is truly not there for you?

This is your life and it hurts even cause you tears. Hence I am the way I am.

I am but a lonely soul waiting to be released from the dungeons of hell.

I am but a lonely soul waiting for the chains of hell to drop off my feet.

All this and more you feel hence the longing for freedom.
The longing for righteousness
Truth
True happiness

I cannot fear man or humanity and what they say or think of me. They're not the ones feeling my pain nor are they the ones living my life.

The journey is long and hard but for some strange reason, I can't give up although I want and need to give up.

Everyone may think it easy and should be easy for me because God – Good God asked me to write a book, but it is so not the case for me. Nothing is given to you on a silver platter. You have to work for it. Find the knowledge and truth in it all. Hence dreams do no walk straight like I've told you.

You have to endure the pain
You have to overcome the physical and spiritual challenges and hurdles including pit falls.

Yes this is my journey, hence I have to live it until I find release or until she comes and save the world. And no I am not John the Baptist, I am MICHELLE JEAN.

November 12, 2013

Yes it's sad but this is my reality.
This is my life story not his story or history.

Yes I would like things to be easy for me but if it's not ordained to be then there is nothing I can do.

Life does have its ups and downs and you have to make life given the struggles and obstacles in your way.

Yes it's easy to give up and giving up is not failure.

You're tired of the closed doors. Plus you are tired physically, mentally and spiritually. You have to take a break and regroup. Do something different and not do the same old same old. You have to get creative. You have to network or even go way back to the days of old when things were original and clean - blessed.

Yes I want to truly leave the publishing company that I am with. I truly need my own company. My own truth that is honest good and true to me.

I need goodness
I need stability
I need true good and positive growth
Honesty

And I so do not have this with this company. This is the way I feel as of late. No, I cannot undo what I've written. I

88

can but I truly don't want or need to hence I will leave well enough alone.

Yes I feel like a number in the grand scheme of things hence all I write after this book I am going to solicit another company in goodness and in truth.

I am tired of closed doors. Had too many lies told to me.

I need goodness to surround me hence I truly need to go back to my roots and let true goodness happen to me.

I truly need Good God to bless me and open up good doors for me, but in my present state it cannot happen because of the negativity that truly surrounds me.

Michelle Jean
November 12, 2013

Winter is fast approaching and it's getting cold outside and inside.

Body rejecting the heavy foods
It seems my body just want things that are light like crackers and cheese.

Can't take the meat, too harsh on the body; it's as if my body cannot tolerate it, can't take the harshness of it – meat.

It's like meat has no taste
Can't stand eating at fast food joints anymore
I don't know but as of late I find the food nasty

Maybe it's just me but the growth hormones and chemicals they put in everything, my body is rejecting and it's only a matter of time when the chemicals and growth hormones truly turn back and bite humans one way or another.

You of yourself must plant truly organic food and fruits.

Good God never ever gave us inorganic anything. Humans are the ones to taint the goodness Good God has and have given us.

You of yourself must take care of your body. No one is going to take care of it for you. You have to do it and live.

You must detoxify the body to get rid of the soot that's built up in the body.

Yes you can fast but not for religious reasons hence fasting with pure and clean drinking water is good. Meaning you must drink water to flush the soot out.

Yes things are coming to an end.

Animals are becoming extinct more and more. So what say man – humanity when all is gone?

They will starve and they too will become extinct leaving an empty planet void of all human beings. And rightfully so because we created this mess that we live in hence we have to live in it. We have to bare the consequences because Good God never told us to destroy everything in sight leaving self and people including land, animals and trees homeless – without a home.

We have to bare the consequences because we took without truly replenishing. Hence earth has become over populated with wicked and evil beings that live to fight, kill and spread hate.

Michelle Jean
November 12, 2013

The body is getting tired Good God and I so don't want to write.

I want to sleep
Need to cuddle up to someone

I am tired
So tired
I have to go to my bed.

In fact I am going to my bed
I need to rest

I need my sleep

Michelle Jean
November 12, 2013

Wow nothing to write
Nothing to say
I am tired and I am so going to bed

Goodnight God – Good God
Goodnight World
Goodnight Mother Earth
Goodnight people of the world – earth

Stay blessed and true to self – yourself
May God – Good God bless you all as well as return all evil back
to sender so that no evil may harm you.

Good God you are mighty and true hence I look to you for all
that is good and true. Thank you God and Good God for blessing
me with Mother Earth and my family including your family.

Thank you for Good Life
Good everything

Truly thank you for blessing Mother Earth with an abundance of
food and water.

Truly thank you for the trees and water you've given me upon
the earth.

I truly love you and once again, truly thank you for the goodness
you've given me on earth, in the spiritual realm including the
goodness and truth in your good abode.

Michelle Jean
November 12, 2013

Dear God earth is being ravished because the water comes and no one is safe from the pending destruction of man – humanity.

Wow. What does 2014 and beyond hold for me Good God?

Speaking about that, 2014, I did something wrong today and got caught. Hence I can't get a break or a bly from you.

But truly thank you for giving me a nice bus driver that let me off without embarrassing me.

Also, truly thank you to the bus driver.

So God – Good God, how come I can't do wrongs but yet others can do wrong each and every day without getting caught? Years upon years pass by and they don't get caught.

This is a double standard on your part. And don't you even dare smile at me because you are not fair.

Evil and wicked people get away with so much including murder and I can't get away with one wrong. I know, I know wrong is wrong when it comes to your children but you still have a double standard this according to me.

I am going to say this now and please excuse me and forgive me for these words because I know I am wrong but I *am going to say these words anyway. In my view you are two faced just like man.*

No, no, no, no, no. Well yes you can be angry at me for calling you two faced and I know you are angry at me. But truly look at the way wicked and evil people manipulate the system and even kill and they get away with it. Some even write their own laws to justify their wrongs. A prime example of this is the book of sin – man's so called holy bible. So tell me Good God, how are you fair? Yes I know these people are not your people but the devil's own because many kill to maintain their millions and billions. But Good God did the devil create earth? The devil did not did he? So why are you providing a home for her children and his children?

Yes life is life but when did you become responsible for wicked and evil life?

Many have sacrificed their souls as well as the souls of others to keep their wealth and place in hell. Now tell me Good God, how fair and just are you to your people when evil has and have captured it all and is destroying it all?

How fair are you to your people when your people have to live amongst wicked and evil people?

How is that true love? Is that not hatred of your own?

Michelle Jean November 13, 2013

God – Good God, I am going to take a page out of Ity and Fancy Cat's comedy skit now and ask, "How Could You?"

How could you, when you knew and know how destructive evil is?

How could you, when you knew and know the pain we would face at the hands of death's children – sin's children?

How could you, when you knew and know that humans – the children of evil would destroy all on earth including your people even you?

God – Good God one act of defiance plunged the earth including the spiritual realm into the utter darkness of hell. This darkness is a blinding light that hinders us from seeing the truth, so how could you?

"How could you?"
"How could you?"
"Truly how could you?"

God – Good God, how do we reclaim earth and stop the destruction of man – humanity?

The West is done. Now they seek to destroy what's left of Africa.

Truly look at what America is doing in Africa and tell me what right do they have to tell Africans how to live and conduct themselves?

Do they not give our people guns and ammunition to kill themselves so they can come in and rape the land? Steal what's left of it?

Do they not steal the resources of Africa and leave the people of Africa to starve and die?

Did they along with other vile nations not introduce AIDS and HIV, Malaria and all manner of infectious diseases to Africa to kill the people then turn around and tell lies on Africa that these diseases come from there?

Hence I ask you yet again how fair and just are you to your people when you of yourself know the lies and deceit of the different nations when it comes to your own? So truly, "how could you."

Evil has and have tried to kill you.
Evil has and have persecuted you.
Evil has and have denied you but yet you maintain and sustain evil and evil has done nothing good for you. Evil is destroying all you have created and built, but yet you stand aside and do nothing for your people.

Evil nailed you to a cross literally (NOT JESUS) but you – your goodness and truth, then have people come into their whore houses called churches to further mock and disgrace you. And you cannot say that I am lying because evil charge 1/10th or 10% (percent) of each individual's wages to keep you down – bring you to hell with them. They mock life – good life which is you in their churches and you cannot say no. You infinitely cannot say I am lying because you know they do. Just look at the spirit of man – the sins of man on a daily basis and tell me otherwise. And you cannot tell me otherwise because you infinitely know that I am correct – right about all of this.

Don't go there because I am pointing at the cross of dead atop the churches as well as inside of them.

I am pointing at the inverted cross and swastika inside some of them. Some are even buried in them.

I am pointing at the cross of death that is on the tombstones and casket of the wicked and innocent in cemeteries.

I am pointing at the six pointed stars that are encased and shrined in synagogues and some churches.

I am pointing at the inverted triangle and the mocking of the upright triangle by sins children. So

*you cannot say I am wrong when you infinitely know
I am right – correct.*

*You have to secure Africa for your African people –
children because it is not right for the Americans or the
Europeans – anyone for that matter to come back into
Africa and destroy it all. And no I will not plea for
Ethiopia. I refuse to. I do not hate them but I refuse to plea
for them.*

*You gave us Africa as our birthright and no other nation
has or have the right to come in and destroy it. Come on
now. You cannot abandon your children like a dead beat
dad. Come on now. I am pleading for Africa because South
Africa is our right and you infinitely know this. Hence I
have to plea for them Africa but not Ethiopia.*

*What right does anyone have to destroy Africa?
What right do you as God and Good God have to let anyone
do so – destroy Mama Africa?*

Yes I am being bold but I have to ask you these questions.

**South Africa is the womb of life – the Cradle of Life
so how come you are allowing Non Africans
including so called Africans to rob and destroy the
Cradle of Life?**

*Trust me the East will become the same shortly if they
don't smarten up because it seems like the Philippines is*

nestled on the chopping block. Meaning from my perspective, it's a matter of time before that land truly sinks. **_This is my perspective Good God from what I see. Hence do not quote me. I am just telling you what I see. Not what you've given me to see and say._**

I've asked you nicely to spare Kenya and China because of Lucy and Eva. This is due to their kindness and goodness bestowed upon or unto me and my children and you refuse to listen to me.

Now I ask you again, "How Could You?" Stop death from chopping down Kenya and China. I asking you nicely because these two people (Eva and Lucy) did show me kindness and you have to spare their homeland. They did not do to get. They showed true love and true care hence you have to show Kenya and China true love and true care because of goodness. Remember, one act of true kindness is all it takes and you got that, so truly protect China and Kenya in truth of me and you.

Jamaica failed you but am I failing you?

I need the island (Jamaica) to be cleaned up infinitely and indefinitely forever ever yes and I will not stand in death's way of doing his and her job. Death must take her and his obeah working, backbiting, backstabbing, entitlement attitude, rapist, pedophile, incest rectobate, murderess, Satan loving (church going) people with them because the people of the land has and have turned Judah into the modern day Sodom and Gomorrah. *Jamaica must be destroyed worse than Port Royal of 1692 and the Philippines of modern day. I will feel sorry for none of my people because I know the wickedness of them hence I do not plea for them, I plea for the land itself because the land did you nothing.* The people did you wrong but the land did you nothing. You cannot punish the land for what man – humans have done. It is not fair to the land, hence I say you are unjust. Man – humans made the land unclean not the land made the land unclean so it is humans that must be punished. Good Life should not have to suffer for the ills and wickedness of man – wicked and evil people. If I am wrong say I am wrong because I know you truly have a voice to speak.

Like I've said, from Eve slap back to now we as Black People have not learnt hence we disappoint you daily.

We have not learned to walk away from the devil's seed – children. We wine and dine with them plunging ourselves closer and further into hell.

We must stop but we refuse to. **I learnt my lesson hence my hardships and pain.**

I've asked you to forgive me but forgiveness is not forth coming. I've caused you pain hence I am living in pain.

I know the realm of death and evil and I strive not to go there. I need to be in your good and true abode but you need to help me as well as help your people. We cannot do this without you nor can we do this without your knowledge. We have to know you hence you have to let us in. Give us the necessary information and tools to regain your trust – you.

We've all sinned Good God and the reign of terror by evil's children must stop. You have to put a stoppage to the madness of earth.

Look at earth now and truly tell me if this was what you wanted for man? Is this what you want for earth?

Look at the slaughtering of men women and children and tell me if this is what you wanted for man – humans.

I know the book of sin said you told your prophet to kill man woman and child. But Good God this is not you and I know this. The book of sin otherwise known as the holy bible is not your book because you did not commission anyone to write it. *You would not take life because you are not death. Hence I tell you, let death have his and her children. They are not your own and it is not right for you to be protecting them like I've said.*

What does not belong to you does not belong to you.

*You as Good God cannot fight for what does not belong to you. **If you do then I can say Good GodF meaning you failed.***

Death's children are not your children so stop holding out on change when it comes to sinful and wicked people. I learnt the hard way and you have to hence it's time for us to let go. If a man does not want change you cannot force him to change.

If a man or woman including child do not truly love you, you cannot force him or her to do so – truly love you.

If a man or woman including child do not care for you or about you, you cannot force him or her to do so – truly care for you.

If a man or woman including chid refuse you, let them go their way because they are telling you they don't want or need you. They don't care, so truly leave them the hell alone. You are not a beggar so do not beg humanity anything. If humanity fail to listen not just in voice but in songs – words then leave them alone. You did your job as a father. Now it's time to leave humanity alone like you left Evening alone. But in truth you did not leave Evening alone and this has to do with the Night. For which I have not touched on because Night is not easily explained.

If a man is dirty you cannot force him to be clean. You cannot continue to go against the good will of your people because you are hurting us in the process.

Sin had its time and his time as well as her time is up. Now sin and the children of sin must go to death. They must go and live in their father's home which is hell. This was the deal. Now let me remind you of this. Hence let the will of evil be done by giving death his pay.

Remember, "THE WAGES OF SIN IS DEATH." So why are you blocking death from truly taking her and his own.

You know the law hence you have to abide by the law.

Like I said, we all make mistakes but if we continue to sin willfully then death must take us. Come on now. Sin's children are no exception to the law, so why are you making them an exception?

You have nothing to do with death so stop protecting the children of the dead. Come on now. Who have you killed?

Who have you slaughtered?

Sin slaughtered, hence they have their holy bible to teach humanity how to slaughter, rape, murder, steal and do all that is sinful – wrong. The Holy Bible is sin's book hence humanity use it to sin and spread lies as well as tell lies.

Humans think this book is from you when it is infinitely and indefinitely forever ever not from you but from sin.

LIFE CANNOT BE DEATH *even I know this. Come on now.*

The children of the dead did not choose you. Now look at the planet earth. Right can infinitely never ever be wrong. So why are you making yourself wrong?

Why are you allowing the children of the dead to destroy earth and all you've created including you?

Why are you allowing your children to mingle and suffer with death's children?

And more importantly, why are you not defending Mother Earth and her children?

How can you say you love us so and neglect land – Earth?

Is earth not a part of man? And don't you dare say how because the flesh is the same makeup as earth and the spirit is the same makeup of your energy. So don't you dare go there lest I go ballistic on you. And don't you dare say men fell from grace hence they became fleshy because I know otherwise hence the XY and not XX. Remember I know you and I know the spiritual world hence the spiritual world is not easily explained if you do not know it.

As Bob Marley say, you can fool some of the people sometime but you can't fool all the people all the time.

As Marcus Mosiah Garvey sey, if yu no noa wey yu a cum from how yu a go noa wey yu a go? So truly don't because no one can fall from grace. I know this now. Absolutely no one can fall from grace if you do not have grace. We leave your fold for something else. We're deserters hence backbiters and giver backer takers. Hence love and not true love have we.

You cannot say you are right when humanity is living wrong.

You cannot say you are right when I am living wrong and in need of guidance, true happiness, true love and all that is good honest and true from you.

I cannot give you right when you are wrong because you have neglected earth.

You have neglected the animals and creatures of earth.

Tell me, how many animals and creatures have and has become extinct because of the wickedness of man – humanity?

Now tell me this Good God, what have you done and what did you do to truly save them (these animals and creatures) from extinction?

You are so busy worrying about man and saving man – humans but in all you did, you became the neglectful one.

The animals of earth became the neglected ones.
Earth became the neglected one.
The waters of earth became the neglected ones.

Remember you gave them good life, so why allow the dead to destroy and kill them?

Do humans not steal their space and destroy them in the process? So how can we as humans say we are life when we cannot even share? We are the true destructive and deceitful ones.

You Good God are doing nothing to save the animals of the land.

You did nothing to maintain and sustain their homes. So tell me, how just are you?

How fair are you to the good animals of the land?

So, "HOW COULD YOU?"

Truly, "HOW COULD YOU?"

Truly look at the earth Good God and tell me Michelle if what humans do to earth, the creatures and animals of the earth including humans is just?

Why do you not cry for Mother Earth and help her Good God?

Humans are killing her (earth) and all you do is stand aside and look. Watch as we kill her (earth) more and more. Well I am pleading for Mother Earth and the animals including trees and water.

You cannot let humans continue to destroy and kill her. She was here long before humans came about. You have a right and obligation to her because she did you no wrong.

Earth – Mother Earth have to put up with our crap literally and never one day has complained to you.

I've never seen it Good God and if she has, she has not told me nor do I know. So look at her as well and truly help her. She deserves your help because she is putting up with us including enduring our disrespect of her.

She too needs you. The trees and water including the animals need you. So what say you?

Do you value humans over her? Come on now. Earth has life so why are you allowing humans to destroy her. I have yet to see an animal lift up arms against earth but humans lift up arms against her on a daily basis. Now tell me who is deserving of earth including you?

Who is deserving to be called your own?

Tell me now, who is the civilized ones Humans or Animals?

Like I said, right can never ever be wrong, so why are you living wrong and making yourself out to be wrong?

Michelle Jean November 13, 2013

Wow sorry Good God because I went right into you. I never even said, "Good Morning."

Well Good God, good morning and have a blessed and prosperous day.

Yes Michelle is at it again but I can't help it this is me. I have to keep you on your toes because somehow you needed this. To be honest, I think you get a high and or rush when I challenge you like this.

Humans are the destroyers.

We build to suit self hence destroying all that is insight and this cannot be.

Listen you may not like me but you have to truly love me.

Hey, I am truly here for you and I am hoping you are truly there for me as well.

God – Good God, I cannot just cry out for people without crying out for Mother Earth and her children – the trees and water including animals. And yes the air too because I've neglected the air hence Air I am truly sorry for neglecting you.

Tell me something Good God, what right does humanity have to take at will without replenishing what they have taken?

What right does anyone or any human have to put the earth at risk like this?

We cannot create but yet we destroy.

Don't even go there because if we could create, we would have created good life as well as recreate what we have destroyed.

Man is not you Good God remember that. So man cannot pass dem place when we pass filth, Nana, Kaka from our bodies literally. We stink period. I know you did not make us stink. Our sins and the filth that we eat make us stink literally.

So since we cannot create, you cannot allow us to continue to destroy. It is not right nor is it fair and just to earth. You have to do something to protect her and one of the things you need to do is to give death his people and let them be gone from earth infinitely and indefinitely forever ever. Death's children or the children of the dead must never ever come back to earth for more than infinite and indefinite forever ever lifetimes and generations.

Give death is own because you are contributing to the problem. The time of sin is up hence **GOOD MUST RECLAIM HER OWN AND LIVE FOREVER EVER IN GOODNESS AND IN TRUTH.**

Michelle Jean November 13, 2013

So for you that are saying you did not clear up anything. I did you just want to know about the afterlife and if there is life after death – the death of flesh.

Once again:

THERE IS NO LIFE AFTER DEATH FOR THE WICKED AND SINFUL MAN – EVIL.

If you did not live a clean and true life on earth you cannot live a true and clean life in the grave because there is no life in the grave.

How can I explain it? The grave is your court house. Where you go for sentencing or where you go to know your fate.

So if you have more bad than good you will infinitely never ever see Good God. Meaning your triangle is turned down and you will go down to see Death. You are going to die a painful death in hell.

If you have more good than bad then you will go up to see Good God. You have nothing to worry about when the spirit sheds the prison – the flesh.

KNOW THAT THE FLESH IS A PHYSICAL PRISON FOR THE SPIRIT.

NOW YOU KNOW ABOUT PHYSICAL PRISON. THERE IS A SPIRITUAL PRISON AS WELL. THIS WE CALL HELL AND THE CONTAINMENT UNITS IN HELL HAS FIRE, ATOMIC FIRE AS I CALL IT.

This is the place you don't want to get to because it is that deadly. Billions are going to go there because billions have and has defiled the body with body art and or Tattoos.

HENCE THE MARK OF THE BEAST THAT BILLIONS SO WILLINGLY ACCEPT WITHOUT KNOWING IT.

Go back to the book of sin. It said God put a mark on Cain that anyone that see him would not kill him. Like I've told you CAIN HAD THE MARK OF HIS FATHER WHICH WAS AND IS THE MARK OF DEATH.

Good God does not mark anyone for death, you are born with the mark of death and I've told you what that mark is in my other books. We as humans also accept the mark of the beast and that mark in our day and time are tattoos and henna.

To put any form of mark, whether it be tattoos or henna on your skin is an infinite sin. Cuts are different people so please do not bring cuts and bruises into this lest I be angry. Belly rings and or navel rings – piercings are different. This includes ear piercing. Any other piercings are infinitely and indefinitely wrong. If I am wrong about

113

belly or navel including ear piercing, I will let you know. So for now hold on to those as being okay. And if Good God tell me I am wrong and that navel or belly piercing including ear piercing is wrong I will let you know. And yes Good God I will accept wrong and accountability for this. So truly do not punish the people that will now go out and get navel and or ear piercing. Yes I am taking responsibility Good God and you have this book as my record of truth. So I cannot change my word or say I did not say so.

Michelle Jean
November 17, 2013

Onwards I go because I toggle between dates.

Dear God truly help me in a positive way and good morning to you.

A blessed morning to you because the spiritual war is brewing. Yet again this morning, I dreamt I was on a spaceship that was in battle or at war.

I keep seeing this spiritual fight Good God and humans are dying. This man was cut in half. This fight is not pretty hence I so do not know what to do. I do not know how to decipher these spiritual war dreams hence I am going to leave them alone because the fighting is not done on earth. Many are going to die because this is truly the last of days for humanity.

I cannot say rescue me or rescue humanity because we've put the earth – world at risk with our sins.

I cannot say rescue me or rescue humanity because we've put the earth – world at risk and destroyed her for personal gain. Earth need to be vindicated hence I tell you yet again, return the evils of man – humanity back to sender and let them – humans feel the pain.

I will not cry for them because in all humans do, they destroy and kill.

Earth does not deserve the wicked treatment she's getting from man – humanity.

*The trees and water including the air and animals do not deserve the wicked and evil treatment of man – humanity. Hence I will not cry for man – humanity but for the sake of truth and honesty, **SPARE CHINA, KENYA; THE SOUTHERN LANDS OF AFRICA INCLUDING JAMAICA BUT NOT THE WICKED AND EVIL PEOPLE OF JAMAICA. SPARE SCOTLAND DUE TO ANCESTRAL LINEAGE maybe Russia if they do not change. Please do not ask me why Russia because you know I have a soft spot for them for some strange reason hence I put them in lower case and not upper case. And people please do not ask me about the casing.***

Once again spare the land of Jamaica – the land of my birth because I truly love my homeland. Spare the land but not the wicked and evil people that live there. They have and has done worse than abominable acts of sin under your GOOD AND TRUE NAME AS WELL AS ON LAND.

This morning in my dream of Jamaica the pool water was clean and clear. I saw the image of birds in the water hence I am going to play THREE LITTLE BIRDS by Bob Marley.

The water, pool water was clear and pretty – clean. The dream had to do with Mark Myrie's son. He is the son of jailed Jamaican artist Buju Banton. In the dream someone was singing for Buju Banton. A fight broke out between

Buju's son and someone and Buju's son kicked his ass meaning won the fight. As for the birds that were in the water. They were not live birds but painted birds like the twitter bird. I don't know if the birds in the water represent the innocent lives that have been taken in Jamaica but I think it does but I am not sure. Hence I am correlating this dream with what I said above in regards to the creep that posted naked pictures of underage boys on twitter with semen on one of them.

And thank you to the lone knight that reported this creep to twitter. May Good God truly bless you abundantly with the good riches and wealth of his abode. You truly helped because I sent direct messages to people of influence that could help and they did nothing. So once again truly thank you. And Good God truly remember the goodness of this man hence I am asking you in goodness and in truth to let this act of goodness wipe out all his wrongs and his families wrongs so that they can get to your good and true abode when the time comes. Truly thank you for what he did Good God because he helped in a good and true way hence I truly and truthfully plead for him and his family when death comes to take his and her own.

I do hope twitter follow up on it because I am sure these children are a part of someone's sick and cruel sex trade organization. I am also hoping that the police thoroughly investigate this incidence and charge the necessary parties including twitter if it has to.

Social media is not a game and people should not be exposed to seeing disgusting half naked selfies of people who do not respect themselves.

If you want to post half naked selfies then post it on a porn web site.

*Underage children are on twitter and they follow us. **So to all my underage followers, I do apologize for you seeing my cussing tweet to this creep that posted the disgusting pictures of naked boys.***

Like I said, we have no morals or values anymore when we as adults and young adults participate in immoral activities. These children don't know better because you can clearly see from the photo they learnt this from an adult. An adult taught them to do this hence the sick and disgusting things our children are doing. Hence I call upon you now Good God to INFINITELY AND INDEFINITELY MAKE EVERY PARENT, GOVERNMENT, FAMILY MEMBER ACCOUNTABLE FOR OUR CHILDREN OR THEIR CHILDREN. Meaning Good God, we cannot see our children doing wrong and continue to condone the bad behaviour. We are *to teach them right from wrong **and yes I know we can't see what they are doing outside the home. I know many are influenced by friends and they don't listen.** I am going through the not listening as well as the nasty phase or stage with my children hence I bug Good God so much about them. I am talking about parents, strangers even social media, Internet providers, law enforcers, politicians, judges, doctors, family, parents, teachers, priest, all members of the clergy that condone and participate in this nastiness of selling children and putting them in sex shops, movies, work houses you name it. Good God, I need you to truly handle this and take charge of this by any means necessary. These children need a strong and good voice and I infinitely and indefinitely forever ever need you to be their strength and voice. Come on now.*

What does it profit anyone to go down in hell? Like I said, hell will be unleashed on earth real soon and what say man – humanity when they can't find food, medicine and water to eat or drink?

I hope when the pain of hell is unleashed on us we truly think of what we have done to others, our children, other people's children, country, self and Good God including Earth and the goodness of earth.

LET'S PUT IT THIS WAY, IF YOU THINK IT'S HELL NOW, TRULY WAIT UNTIL TOMORROW.

119

ONWARDS I GO.

At the end of the dream this young man asked – said, "If it does not hurt Jah to see what we have become?"

So now God – Good God, I am asking you this question yet again. As taken from the book of sin. Does it not hurt you, truly hurt you to have made man?

Does it not hurt you, truly hurt you to see what human beings have and has become?

Does it not hurt you, truly hurt you to see what human beings are doing to self, land and earth – each other?

Does it not hurt you, truly hurt you to see human beings that cannot create or properly clean self destroy earth and all that you've created?

Does it not hurt you, truly hurt you to know and see humans worshipping the devil – evil, giving the devil – evil all their glory and not giving you any praise – thanks for all the goodness you have given to them?

Tell me something God and Good God, where are your tears?

Where are your tears of sorrow to know that humans have no true love of you or for you?

Yes I know your tears and sorrows because I know your pain hence these books.

I know your shame and disgrace because of man – humans. Hence I know your tears, your joy and your sorrows. Just know that I am truly there for you so weep no more. Better must come for you one day. I know this and I truly claim this for you in goodness and truth.

Dry your tears because someone truly loves you despite the heartache and pain I've caused you including my doubts of you.

This morning truly forgive me. Let's dry each other's tears so we can weep no more.

Let true happiness flow and come so we can wash away our pain and sorrow. Truth and true love is what we truly need. So truly take my hand this morning because I am truly with you and truly there for you.

In all that I do in kindness and goodness of you Good God, I have to get you to think. I have to get you to think hence now I plea to you for Buju Banton – Mark Myrie. I do not know the full circumstances behind his imprisonment. I know it had to do with Driver. If he is truly innocent of the charges laid upon him by man, let him go free.

America cannot speak for anyone nor can their justice system speak for anyone when their justice system is unjust and dirty – unclean.

Their country is unclean; filthier than Jamaica. Hence this morning Allelujah I say unto you AMERICAF. The United States of AmericaF. They have failed you hence Marcus Mosiah Garvey must be vindicated. He delivered your message to them Good God and they destroyed his character. So truly give Marcus Mosiah Garvey justice because a nation of vipers – snakes cannot be just nor are they just. They can only be unjust and America is truly the Snake of the Garden of Eden and you know this because they gave up their place with you.

*England is also the snake of the Garden of Eden but England is a bigger snake. They are the largest snake and the biggest snake of the Valley of Death because it was an Englishman who commissioned the Book of Sin to be written to deceive and kill humanity. **More importantly tell lies about you as well as class you as a murderer and giver backer taker of all.** HENCE ENGLANDF INFINITELY AND INDEFINITELY. Allelujah justice, justice dear God justice. We truly want and justice now.*

My ancestors need to be vindicated Good God. Murder is murder and my Scottish ancestors cannot wait any longer. They need to rest. They must rest in peace. I must rest because the BLOOD OF MY ANCESTORS FLOW DEEPLY THROUGH ME and I cannot take the cries of their pain any longer. My body cannot take it Good God. You cannot let England and the Monarchy of Death feast on our flesh and drink our blood any longer with their book of sin – lies.

Arica, the land you have given us as a home need to vindicated. Your people need to be vindicated. We need a true home hence every child of death – the dead (wicked and evil people) must be evicted from earth immediately. They must go down in flames like America because that land is the seat of deceit and whoredom right now.

America is not innocent so duly and truly evict them out of African lands. We as black people need to clean ourselves up and respect self. We must now truly listen and come off the devil's train.

We need you Good God. We need your truth and peace.

We need your true love and honesty. The blood of my ancestors and people cry out to you dear God; please give them justice especially Marcus Mosiah Garvey because what was done unto him was not right nor was it just. My Scottish ancestors, African ancestors, Jamaican ancestors and Buju Banton (Mark Myrie if he's innocent) need justice.

Look at the way America treat Black People on a whole and tell me if they are just. They say they have a Black President but yet blacks are slaughtered at will. With all *this happening to our black people Good God, I don't know why we are not opening up our eyes and leaving the damned country for greener and better pastures. Why are we staying in lands that care not for us? I won't even talk about the President of the United States of America because he has and have failed you. He truly failed you and his people including his African ancestors. **So I worry not about him because all that has and have turned against you is hell bound right now.** There is no saving grace for them, truly no saving grace for them hence America, The United States of America, England, Israel and all the kingdoms of earth that has and have joined the Babylonian Empire – Devil's Domain in the spiritual realm and physical realm including the wicked and evil people of the devil's domain including Babylonian domain in the spiritual and physical realm F. They have been marked F for Fail and Fall Good God, so let death take his own because the law clearly states, "THE WAGES OF SIN IS DEATH," and I am going by the law of Death.*

Yes, Allelujah, Allelujah, Praise your holy and true name Good God. Allelujah. Thank you God and let thy will be done in accordance to the law of Life – Good Life and the law of Death – the Dead.

Praise be to you Good God. America and Israel and all the lands of the devil are going down to hell; must go down to hell and burn for all eternity. They must fall thus saith the Lord thy God meaning it is so.

They have done wickedness in thy sight hence Babylon your kingdom is falling. Must fall because England Allelujah. Yes God, praise be unto you Good God. England must go down to hell and burn with them. America and Israel – all the lands of the devil along with his people must fall and go down to hell for all eternity to burn then eventually die.

A land that kill and persecute the innocent is not holy it is truly sinful. Infinitely and indefinitely not of you Good God.

A land that manufacture guns and weapons; arms to kill another human being including animals is not holy but sinful. They are infinitely and indefinitely not of you Good God but of the devil and his true seeds – race of people.

A land that tell lies; give the people the meat of swines to eat in their lies is not holy but sinful. They are infinitely and indefinitely not of you Good God but of the devil and his true seeds – race of people.

A land that has no good family values is not holy but truly sinful. Hence they are not of Good God.

*A land that turns their children into whores and prostitutes; harlots, beggars and thieves are not holy but truly sinful. **(Remember children are a blessing in many ways and we are to teach them to walk*** *upright in goodness and in truth Good God. This is the law and you know it.)*

Hence many that have sold their children will find no peace in hell because their torment and pain will be greater than the buyer – the one they sold their child to.

So Good God, if we turn our children into the ungodly ones, how can you truly bless us when we including our children are riddled in sin?

We say our children are a blessing but yet we turn them into all that is sinful. So how are they a blessing?

How are we good parents?

How are we good citizens in the eyes and sight of Good God when we do all these sinful things.

A land that gives their children drugs to take cannot charge a next man or anyone for crimes – unlawful crimes because the government of the land do the same except on a mass scale. Hence the guilty cannot charge the guilty for sin or of sin. It is unjust, unlawful and sinful.

A land that send their soldiers to war and kill others cannot charge another land for crimes against humanity because that land too have committed grave acts of sin in the eyes and sight of God – Good God. Hence the guilty cannot charge the guilty of sin. It is the law of God – Good God but yet humanity does not follow this law. Humanity goes against this law each and every day.

America truly look at your young entertainers that glorify drugs and do take drugs. What example are they setting for the global community on a whole?

What example are they setting for the younger generation and future generations to come? Future generations that are global.

Your land has and have become the center of whoredom and nastiness hence your whoredom spread globally through entertainment. Hence many are Satan's gestures in his courts of clowns.

Look at the disrespect of other nations by your young entertainers and tell me if your land is any good?

You picked up where the harlot (England) left off, so tell me, what have you done for Good God to favor you or even save you?

These entertainers are your addicts that are selling your product (drugs) to other nations to screw up their lives. So tell me now, how are you holy and who gave you the right to speak and act for anyone including country when you rape your land and people of their God given rights to life?

127

Look at your national deficit.

Look at all your artists including rap artists that glorify drugs and killing.

Look at your treatment of blacks in the land.

Now tell me who is doing the bidding of the devil?

WHO'S THE DEVIL'S BITCH RIGHT NOW?

Whose whoring themselves on the behalf of the devil and can't get their National Deficit down to a suitable amount – norm?

Many billionaires and millionaires have you, but yet they cannot help you. They cannot pay down your deficit. Know it's only a matter of time before they too become penniless like the land – country.

Good God I am coming directly to you for help. Because of the nastiness of the devil's clan keep them the hell out of Mama Africa. Truly let Africans learn and listen and break away from the United States of America as well as all Babylonian lands – the devil's lands.

Let us truly walk away from them and truly give all of these evil lands back their money.

Let none of your land and lands be indebted to the devil ever again.

Let Africa become truly organic and give back the devil their genetically modified foods and people.

You gave us truly organic foods and water including air and trees. You did not give us surgically modified anything nor genetically modified anything to kill land – earth and self.

Truly take your children and people back Good God because I am truly with you.

We do not need screwed up or conditioned societies anymore.

We need the truth so truly send back – return evil to their wicked and evil land and lands. (Sender)

Wake up the black man literally Good God because we need you hence we must come home to you in order to be saved.

Michelle Jean November 14, 2013

It's the morning yet again Good God and true blessings and peace be with you on this day.

Good prosperity and good wealth be with you always Good God.

True peace and blessings be with you. I wish I had a coffee to give you but I have none. I have not made any yet. Soon I will and knowing me I will drink it all without thinking of you or even sharing it with you.

But take my hand it's outstretched to you. Squeeze it and know that I truly, truly, infinitely truly, truly love you true.

Michelle Jean
November 14, 2013

Oh Lord have mercy
GOOOOOOD – Good God, my birthday is coming up
soon.

What are you going to get me?

What are you going to buy me?

A vacation in South Africa will do. You know I am not
going to stop bugging you about South Africa. Yes I
wanted to go to Cuba but seeming it's you and you are my
true love I want and need to go to South Africa with you.

Yes Lesotho will do because I truly want to go there. But if
Lesotho is not on your radar – map, then Swaziland or even
Zambia will do. I am not picky when it comes to the
Southern lands of Africa but not Ethiopia. Will never ever,
infinitely never ever go there not that I want to. So that
land is off limits to me and your people. Yes this is my
wish.

Now that I've said that. I'm giving you plenty of time to
save up some money because all expenses must be paid by
you.

So truly start saving because I so want and need for you
and me to truly have some fun and play.

MJL – Michelle Jean
November 14, 2013

A blessed and prosperous morning to you Good God.

I have to let you know that I am so disappointed in you this morning because of yesterday.

Not one catch Good God
Not one

Where am I going wrong?
What am I doing wrong?

Am I that much of a pit bull that I scare everyone including you?

Wow, I never knew my persona was that fierce and threatening.

No one even sat beside me on the train and it was full going down.

Oh well that's what I get for truly loving you. I scare people hence the on guard and unfriendly pit bull persona.

Michelle Jean
November 15, 2013

I have to talk Good God because this is the way I feel.

I have to tell you the truth because I am truly disappointed in you.

I'm disappointed in me too hence I have to be me.
I have to recoil and go further into my empty shell.

I am truly not a people person nor do I want or need to be.

I am an introvert hence I have to recoil in me.
I have to recoil in my own little world and truly stay there.

I have to be truly me.
Never was a people person nor can I be. My books – our books are my people, hence I will stay writing them no matter how you disappoint me.

What was I thinking going out in the world hoping I could meet people or meet that right someone. All I get is disappointment hence the true introvert in me.

Michelle Jean
November 15, 2013

Wow I am old and withered
I truly feel out of place because of my gray hair and old fashioned dress – clothes.

I so can't believe just how old I fell and look in reality.
No one shares my interests hence I am alone and miserable on some days.

I want to do all the things that are bad now but I truly can't because badness is so not me. And in truth, I can't stand the smell of stench when it comes to badness – evil.

One sin for the day was enough hence I have to leave humanity alone.

I have to admit I like going out but loathe going out by myself. No one talks to you and I am so not an outgoing person. No, will never go up to a stranger and strike up a conversation. So not in me to do hence it is so not me. I am but a spectator looking in not just in the physical but in the spiritual real at times.

Trust me things take time for me hence sometimes I wonder if I am truly cursed.

Oh well this is the life of me. The waiting game and Good God truly ignoring and avoiding me.

Michelle Jean
November 15, 2013

Yes I have to live my life for me.
I have to live it good and clean hence lately I have fallen off the wagon and I so don't give a shit.

I truly don't care anymore because walking a lonely road is depressing and tiring.

I truly hate to walk alone hence I have to do me so Good God truly forgive me.

I am still going to be the introvert but I truly need to have me some fun.

I refuse to let Good God continue to cage me up like a prisoner. I truly have to do me because you Good God is doing you. You do not let anyone cage you so why are you caging me? You are doing you Good God and I so can't live this boring life with you anymore. You are as boring as me if not more hence you do not do anything to make me truly happy.

I want and need to explore different lands and culture. I truly need diversity hence I truly cannot allow you or let you hold me back from doing what I truly need to do in my life. You failed me hence the loneliness in me. I need to be truly happy and I cannot allow you to take my happiness away from me any longer.

Michelle Jean
November 15, 2013

There's more that I want to add to this book by my head is beginning to hurt so I will not add them. I need closure in this book hence I am going to include these dreams. One already came to pass but I am going to tell it to you anyway.

DREAMS

Dear God I don't know what is going on but I have to come to you for salvation. A saving grace because humanity has gone utterly mad.

Good God it's early in the morning and this dream scares me. I truly do not know what to do because I truly need to be in your protective arms right now.

Good God I need you because I don't know what to make of this dream this morning.

My God, My God, please do not forsake me because human life will never be the same again if this is happening.

We've come this far to destroy it all and I cannot comprehend or overstand why.

I can't fully remember the beginning but I think something happened. It was not war but flooding. I think it was flooding because I was not fully penetrating the dream.

Oh man I can't remember if the earth started to give way like the sink holes of Florida. Oh man I can't remember. But like I said it rained. Some places gave way. There wasn't much people in this dream. I don't know what happened but some of us were running and the army came after us. They were firing their guns. Some got shot – caught but me and this Chinese lady and her family never got caught. We kept going – kept running but no bullets hit us.

We were running on restricted property much like Area 51 of the United States. While running we came upon this place. It was more like a sandy beach where the army (government) were leveling the beach with a bulldozer. They were leveling out the sand and you could see the water. The water was not clean. I call it dirty because it looked dirty to me. The water did not look like dirty water that we would typically but of a mushy green but not that green. This beach was fenced off because it was a restricted area – zone. Although the beach was fenced off there were houses, detached houses on the other side of the fence. People lived in them. There was not much people on the other side of the fence so we tried to blend in with them – the people on the other side of the fence. This soldier approached and asked if they had seen us and the people said in unison "we did not see anyone." The people did not give us away but it was what I saw at the opening of the gate leading to the river that scared me. It disturbed me.

The river I can safely say was manmade and this river was designed for Growth Hormones.

I can't tell you what the sign full read but I remember "GROWTH HORMONES" was a part of the sign.

See the people that were on the other side of the fence were made. Meaning given this water. They were being controlled by this water.

Remember the movie the Stepford Wives of a few years back? Well the people were conditioned like the people of this movie. So from this dream and what I see, something is happening that is classified that humans know nothing about. This place I should not have seen in the dream because it was well protected – armed. The soldiers were white and my mind is saying American but I cannot say they were nor can I confirm or tell you the country that this is happening in because I did not see the country. All I know is something is happening with the waterways somewhere on the globe and this is sad. It is not right.

As humans we've come so far to destroy and kill each other for what? Everyone has a right to life and to live and no government should manipulate you or take away your right to freedom.

No government should clone humans because we cannot create only procreate with each other.

No government should put growth hormones in our waterways because Good God gave everything to us pure and clean. Like I said, we are the ones to destroy all that Good God has and have given us.

We don't think of our future nor do we truly think of others.

We are the ones to let sin into our lives and now we are destroying everything in sight as well as around us for sin.

We are the wrong and sinful ones, no one else. We are the destroyful ones no one else.

Good God truly tell me how can you continue to permit these things on earth. Now the waterways is slated to die by the hands of man – humanity. Governments are messing with the water supply.

My God, My God please do not forsake me because greater death will be upon land. Funeral homes will not be able to keep up hence mass graves will be upon land. Many humans will die without a proper burial place. They will become the nameless – unknown just like unknown soldiers of death – War.

Michelle Jean
November 15, 2013

Yes God – Good God, I need death to take his people hence death will now touch the waterways of man – humanity. The Scorpion Kings will walk hence death is destroying all that is in her path. Dry death will be the norm.

What will humanity do?

Many things I see now.

I saw King Kong Good God coming out a picture. He was huge and he was like darkness. So dark I thought he was going to crush me because he walked on land. But I laid down and he stepped over me and I woke up out of my dream. Yes I was scared and this morning I found out a tornado devastated part of the United States.

I dreamt about Oprah, Kendrick Lamar hence Arsenio leave the man alone because in the dream you went on the bash crusade when it came to him not participating in the whoredom of the rap world. You are duly warned. Not everyone is of nastiness. Remember that.

I also dreamt about Will Smith. Will all I have to say to you is. You cannot let your last two children dominate and control you. If you are not happy in a situation walk away in peace – true peace. In doing so still be there for your children because you are being sucked dry literally. That's all I got to say. And this is from the dream. What I saw.

Remember, Good God is the fixer of everything. Trust me, I know the mechanic shop of man and it is filthy. Filled with dirty laundry – car parts. Trust not man because at the end of the day man is going to lose it all and they do fail you.

Walk away in truth not in blindness.

Do not participate in whoredom because you are so not bad from the dream. You are a good person you just have to change the way you do things for the better and better good.

Everyone must do this because like I said, in all the devil stores up, his people will become the biggest losers of them all. They will lose everything including the billions which amounts to trillions that they store up.

THERE IS GOING TO BE A NEW WORLD ORDER. BUT THAT WORLD ORDER IS OF GOOD AND NOT SIN.

KNOW THAT THE ALLOTED TIME – 24000 YEARS THAT SIN GOT TO DECEIVE IS UP.

EARTH IS DYING AND HUMANITY MUST NOW WALK IN GOODNESS AND IN TRUTH IF THEY WANT TO LIVE.

HUMANITY MUST START REPLENISHING THE EARTH INSTEAD OF KILLING EVERYTHING IN SIGHT.

Right now we are killing animals for sport but in all the wickedness that we do to the animals, that wickedness must come back to haunt and kill man.

EVIL MUST BE RETURNED TO SENDER. HENCE WE ALL KNOW THAT KARMA IS A BITCH WHEN IT COMES BACK AROUND.

Like I said, the dead do walk and they do haunt man hence ghosts. They also talk.

Evil do use the dead to turn down and kill. Every Jamaican know this but we laugh and walk away from it – the truth.

So do that which is right because Good God is truly there for you. So truly talk to him what you need and want and he will show you exactly what to do. Not in a bad way but in a good and true way. And note, HE GOOD GOD WILL NEVER EVER, INFINITELY NEVER EVER TELL YOU TO KILL, SO BANNISH THAT THOUGHT FROM YOUR HEAD. May the good grace of Good God be with you and keep you through your ups and downs because you are so going to need him in all of this.

Michelle Jean
November 17, 2013

OTHER BOOKS BY MICHELLE JEAN

Blackman Redemption – The Fall of Michelle Jean
Blackman Redemption – After the Fall Apology
Blackman Redemption – World Cry – Christine Lewis
Blackman Redemption
Blackman Redemption – The Rise and Fall of Jamaica
Blackman Redemption – The War of Israel
Blackman Redemption – The Way I Speak to God
Blackman Redemption – A Little Talk With Man
Blackman Redemption – The Den of Thieves
Blackman Redemption – The Death of Jamaica
Blackman Redemption – Happy Mother's Day
Blackman Redemption – The Death of Faith
Blackman Redemption – The War of Religion
Blackman Redemption – The Death of Russia
Blackman Redemption – The Truth

The New Book of Life
The New Book of Life – A Cry For The Children
The New Book of Life – Judgement
The New Book of Life – Love Bound
The New Book of Life - Me

Just One of Those Days
Book Two – Just One of Those Days
Just One of Those Days – Book Three The Way I Feel
Just One of Those Days – Book Four

The Days I Am Weak
Crazy Thoughts – My Book of Sin
Broken
Ode to Mr. Dean Fraser

A Little Little Talk
Prayers
My Collective
A Little Talk/A Time For Fun and Play
Simple Poems
Behind The Scars
Songs of Praise And Love

Love Bound
Love Bound – Book Two

Dedication Unto My Kids
More Talk
Saving America From A Woman's Perspective
My Collective the Other Side of Me
My Collective the Dark Side of Me
A Blessed Day
Lose To Win
My Doubtful Days – Book One

My Little Talk With God
My Little Talk With God – Book Two

A Different Mood and World – Thinking

My Nagging Day
My Nagging Day – Book Two

Friday September 13, 2013
My True Love
It Would Be You
My Day